REFRACT
HOUSE

CONCEPTUAL
TRAJECTORIES

11 **GREEN MACHINES FOR LIVING**
ILA BERMAN

29 **MICRO-ECOSYSTEMS AND ENERGY LOOPS**
NATALY GATTEGNO

DESIGN
STRATEGIES

49 **BUILDING LIGHT**
ANDREW KUDLESS

TECHNOLOGICAL
SYSTEMS

73 **ENGINEERING FOR OPTIMIZED PERFORMANCE**
TIM HIGHT

79 **CARBON NEUTRAL DESIGN**
KATE SIMONEN

MATERIAL
FABRICATION

101 **CONSTRUCTION INNOVATION**
PETER ANDERSON

117 **MATERIAL ASSEMBLIES**
MATT HUTCHINSON & OBLIO JENKINS

INTRODUCTION
ILA BERMAN, DIRECTOR OF ARCHITECTURE, CCA

Refract House, a joint endeavor between the Division of Architecture at California College of the Arts and the School of Engineering at Santa Clara University, is a full-scale working prototype of a prefabricated solar-powered home, with a sophisticated sensor-informed energy production and distribution system and an innovative thermal building skin. This faculty- and student-generated research and design-build project is the result of a series of multidisciplinary studios dedicated to the architectural design, engineering, fabrication, on-site assembly, and operation of an innovative, compact, energy-efficient house. It was a top award-winning entry in the U.S. Department of Energy's 2009 Solar Decathlon—an international competition sponsored by the DOE's Office of Energy Efficiency and Renewable Energy dedicated to promoting sustainable solar design. Of the 20 international teams competing, Refract House won first-place honors in both architecture and communications, second place in engineering, and third place overall.

Refract House was developed over a two-year period and entailed a series of faculty-led design studios and project management and technology courses within the architecture programs at CCA. The succession of courses emulated the stages through which a comprehensive architectural project is developed. The process moved from schematic design and design development to the production of working drawings and technical specifications, the fabrication of models and full-scale material prototypes, and finally the complete construction of the house led by the student team on the SCU campus. Paralleling, and intricately interwoven with, the architectural process, the engineering team at SCU comprehensively developed all mechanical, solar, electrical, and structural components of the design, working closely with the architectural design team as well as a small network of outside consultants who generously contributed their time and expertise.

The project also involved the detail design and fabrication of all interior components, furniture, and landscape design elements. A graphic design team was responsible for branding, marketing, and communications. In addition, in keeping with the traditional idea that art and life should form an indivisible synthetic unity through the production of the *Gesamtkunstwerk* or total work of art—a concept that originated in the Arts and Crafts movement out of which CCA evolved—the comprehensive architectural and engineering design of Refract House was enhanced by the individually contributed works of students in CCA's Industrial Design, Furniture, Fashion Design, Textiles, Ceramics, Glass, Painting/Drawing, and Illustration programs, each of which supported the final staging of the house on the National Mall in Washington DC. Throughout the timeframe of its development, including its disassembly in California, transportation across the continent, and four-day reassembly on the opposite coast, Refract House involved the concerted collective efforts of more than 100 students and faculty as well as other individuals who substantially contributed to its realization.

As an overview of Refract House, this publication is intended less as a detailed descriptive account of the challenges and intricacies of the project's evolutionary process than as a reframing of the project within the larger context of the conceptual, spatial, technological, and material issues raised by its implementation. These include the different design strategies explored in the development of the project as well as the questions surrounding its material prefabrication, the integration of its technological systems, and their performance. Given that the vast majority of energy consumed within the United States is still being generated by nonrenewable resources and that buildings account for approximately half of this energy use, the importance of exploring alternatives to current architectural design practices that reduce our occupiable footprints and integrate more sustainable systems for energy production and use—one of the primary objectives of the Solar Decathlon competition—would seem to be an imperative within the context of educating the next generation of architects and engineers.

Of course, assessing the environmental impacts of buildings is not limited to operational energy use, but must also account for the embodied energy that is integral to architectural materials, their fabrication, transportation, and modes of assembly during construction, as well as the ways in which they contribute to other environmental effects. For instance, although it was not critical to the terms of the Solar Decathlon, the team made a deliberate decision to employ primarily recycled and renewable materials in the construction of Refract House. This constituted a critical ethical positioning of the project, intended to diminish the quantity of building waste that is currently generating a new form of postindustrial geology in landfill sites across the country. Similarly, the harvesting and recycling of water within the house recognizes the value and scarcity of water, addressing environmental pollution and other global challenges.

These constitute the wider framework within which Refract House was created, and the intention of its designers to generate a more meaningful, compelling, and innovative architectural product that addresses the many complex issues fundamental to sustainable building practices while simultaneously ensuring uncompromised livability and a seamless integration of advanced technology with progressive design.

MILGARD ALUMINUM FIXED
WINDOWS
08 51 13

MILGARD ALUMINUM FIXED
WINDOWS
08 51 13

SWINGING ALUMINUM-
FRAMED GLASS DOORS
08 32 13

MILGARD ALUMINUM OPER-
ABLE WINDOWS
08 51 13

MILGARD ALUMINUM OPER-
ABLE WINDOWS
08 51 13

SOLAR THERMAL SKIRT-
PHOTOVOLTAIC GENERA-
TION
26 31 00

FSC CERT. WOOD RAIN
SCREEN
06 49 00

END CAP

HORIZONTAL LOUVERS
TRACK
08 90 00

MOMENT FRAME
05 12 23.79

RIPARIAN ZONE, VERNAL
STORM OVERFLOW

OUVERS

UM-FRAMED

RAIN CATCHMENT POOL
33 47 00

HYDROZONED VEGETABLE
LANDING
32 91 00

NATIVE CALIFORNIA
GRASSES

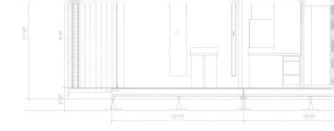

CONCEPTUAL
TRAJECTORIES

GREEN MACHINES FOR LIVING
ILA BERMAN

Our ongoing search for new, more energy-efficient architectural materials, systems, and technologies to support contemporary living continues—yet also directly challenges—a trajectory initiated in the early part of the 20th century, when the revolutionary products of engineering and industry were inspiring new conceptual, spatial, and material models for architecture. The Maison Citrohan of 1921, for example, one of the most infamous architectural products that glorified the industrialization of this era, was introduced by Le Corbusier as a "machine for living in." This house was to be made of standardized industrial components, a kit of parts, whose mode of manufacture and fabrication would emulate modern automobile-industry assembly processes. Perceived to be potentially mobile as it floated above the ground plane—seemingly akin to the French automobile (Citroen) that was its namesake—the Maison Citrohan was intended to be a prototype for modern living that symbolically raised function, geometry, and industry to the level of art.

This progressive emblem of house-as-machine, which found its apotheosis in the Villa Savoye that Le Corbusier built 10 years later, was recontextualized in America as a real product of industry by Buckminster Fuller's designs for the Dymaxion House, developed between 1927 and 1946. These prototypes revolutionized the concept of dwelling by redirecting the technologies of the postwar aircraft industry—in this case lightweight, high-strength aluminum parts of the fuselages of B29 bombers—toward the prefabrication of actual machines for living in. Fuller's pragmatic and positivist approach, which countered Le Corbusier's symbolic and typological branding of a new modern architecture, was an attempt to remobilize and recycle industrial technologies developed for military production in order to attain a new level of construction efficiency within the housing industry that would be technologically advanced, economically accessible, and ecologically responsible.

Fuller's Dymaxion Houses were designed to be off-grid and autonomous, each supported on a single central stainless steel strut that not only connected the building to the ground, but also encased and channeled its internal plumbing and utilities. These "dwelling machines" were also planned to be self-powered and earthquake-proof, with a minimal ecological footprint, each containing its own composting, water collection, and gray water recycling systems. Conceived as a prefabricated industrial product that would harness the latest scientific and technological advances, the first full-scale Dymaxion prototype was intended to redesign not simply the architecture of a single house but the entire construction industry. Fuller, writing in the context of a chronic postwar housing shortage, claimed it would do

nothing less than "re-house the world."[1] Each house enclosed 1,075 square feet of living area, weighed 6,000 pounds (eventually to become 3,000 pounds with advances in material engineering), and cost just $6,500 (for the disassembled "kit"). Despite enthusiastic reviews and overwhelming consumer interest, the Dymaxion House lacked the financial support required for the initial industrial tool-up to put it into mass production and thus was never actualized within the American housing market.

Of course, it was not only for lack of resources that Fuller's invention was not easily incorporated into the architectural fabric of existing society. It was also because of the prototype's resistance to cultural convention and its mechanistic dissociation from the natural landscapes it was meant to occupy. Despite America's enthusiastic acceptance of the machine, it

was perhaps inevitable that people would not feel comfortable truly living within a literal manifestation of it, and that the conflation of domestic architecture with modern technology was destined for a different trajectory. As Leo Marx elaborated in his 1964 book *The Machine in the Garden*, the paradox of the American imaginary, stretched as it was between the utopian pastoral ideal on the one hand and the advance of modern industrialization on the other, embodied a profound contradiction of values, seemingly committed to both a bucolic form of rural happiness and its technocratic antithesis, as evidenced by society's overwhelming desire for industrial productivity and economic wealth. This dichotomy of competing values, and the urge to find a middle ground between the hard social and collective reality of the overcivilized city and the uncertainties of its surrounding wild nature, are in part what led to the American embrace of the suburban landscape. We longed for a more domesticated "natural" environment while simultaneously demanding that this expansive suburban field of individuated dwellings dotting an artificially produced lawnscape be adequately supported by the machine— that is, by the most advanced modern technological amenities.

ABOVE
Detail of salvaged redwood rainscreen and window

OPPOSITE
View of house and deck

Unlike the European mind, which has historically linked advanced civilization to the cultural development of its cities, the American desire to reconnect with an unspoiled virgin territory (as an instantiation of a new, pure beginning for Western civilization) and simultaneously colonize and control the vastness of this undomesticated terrain through an emphasis on the intensive coevolution of agriculture and engineering finds its manifestation in the specificity of its modes of occupying this landscape. In architectural terms, the ideal embodiment of this occupation inevitably returns us to Frank Lloyd Wright's domestic architecture, one that was emblematic of a model of American living understood as deeply connecting a dwelling with the landscape from which it emerged. Wright's Prairie and Usonian Houses, for example, were low-lying, extended horizontal organizations (an emulation of the expansiveness of the American geography and its endless horizon) that incorporated abstract geometries with natural as well as industrial materials, and were defined according to an earthbound syntax that characterized the embedded relationship of these buildings to their sites.

These architectural tactics were intended to produce a specifically American lexicon for the development of domestic architecture in harmony with the landscape, which was then integrated within a larger strategy for collective occupation, as represented by Wright's anti-urban proposal for Broadacre City. Dispersing individuals and buildings across a seemingly endless terrain—the antithesis of the ordered Cartesian social utopias

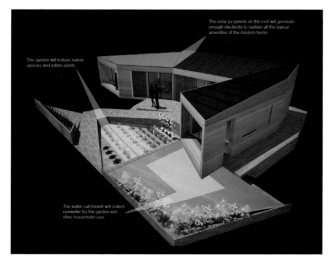

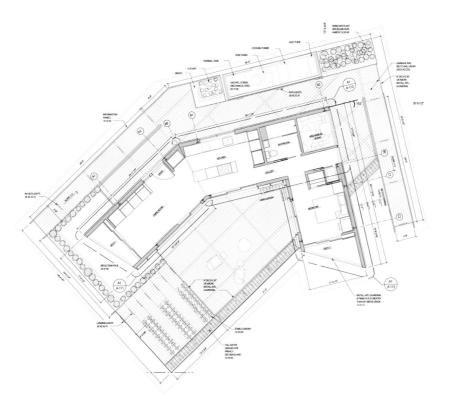

of dense urban living espoused by Wright's European counterparts—the
endless organic patchwork of Broadacre City, and the earlier Jeffersonian
model of land colonization that it referred to, anticipated the suburban attitude toward privatized collective life that would eventually dominate, and
lead to the ubiquity of, American x-urbanism.[2] Wright wrote in 1932 in
his first book on city planning—*The Disappearing City*—that the city should
be everywhere and nowhere, and that it should emerge organically rather
than be planned or designed. The legacy of this is the sprawl that defines
our current suburban condition.

Almost 80 years later, the impact of our uncontained occupation and
industrial instrumentalization of the natural landscape has led to global
warming and the rapid depletion of our natural resources. Like Fuller, we
are now searching for new architectural and engineering solutions to
transform the ways in which we design artifacts for both individual and
collective forms of inhabitation. That the private single-family home, the
cornerstone of the American suburban domestic condition, would become
the building type adopted by the United States Department of Energy for
the Solar Decathlon competition is therefore questionable but certainly

ABOVE
View of outdoor deck, into
interior living area above
water catchment pool

OPPOSITE
View through kitchen into
living area showing large
glazed openings that erase
the boundary between
indoor and outdoor space

not surprising. Although problematic, in that this architectural type rep-resents one of the conditions responsible for our current environmental crisis, perhaps it also represents a starting point from which we must seek a solution to the problems it has engendered, while allowing us to revisit some of the driving principles behind earlier ecological building prototypes. The imperative to look for strategies that support the sustainability of the planet through design—that limit our environmental footprint (perhaps through collective forms of housing rather than individual houses) while also curbing the incessant drive to accelerate the cycle of production and consumption—is certainly among the most important endeavors facing the next generation of architects and designers.

Refract House represents one trajectory in response to this challenge. It is an energy-efficient, prefabricated, solar-powered home—a 21st-century machine for living in, designed to be emblematic of the ideal of contempo-rary California living. Its highly compact enclosed area of 530 square feet is intended to sit lightly upon the Earth, minimizing the carbon footprint associated with environmentally conditioning its enclosed occupiable space while simultaneously expanding into, and becoming a part of, its surrounding landscape. The interior space of the house is both visually and physically continuous with a 700-square-foot deck that defines an occupi-able outdoor courtyard and living space—an artificially constructed topog-raphy that supports an edible garden, a natural water filtration system, and a rainwater catchment and collection system. Since water conservation in California and around the globe is one of our most critical environmental concerns, the water system of the house, which recycles gray water and rain runoff filtered through riparian plants and gravel, includes a catch-

ment system and collection pool. These are part of the building's extended landscape and store water for dry-season garden irrigation.

As with the early houses of Wright, and in response to the ubiquitous desire in California to be directly immersed in the surrounding terrain, the extended linear footprint of the house amplifies its relationship to the ground while wrapping the site in order to partially contain and define its adjacent geography as an expanded, yet delimited, surface for occupation. The small environmental footprint and compressed conditioned space are therefore countered by the expansive perceptual experience of the house as it horizontally migrates into and becomes a part of the landscape. This condition is further facilitated by the subtle erasure of the boundary between interior and exterior spaces through vast openings and glazed transparent surfaces. The idea that this landscape and its larger environment could become reconceptualized as an integrated biotic machine for the production and regeneration of energy and food, and that the remediation and recycling of water could also become part of the extended systems of the house, challenges us to rethink the larger natural and cultural cycles that are conjoined with dwelling, and our impact on and exchanges with our local surroundings.

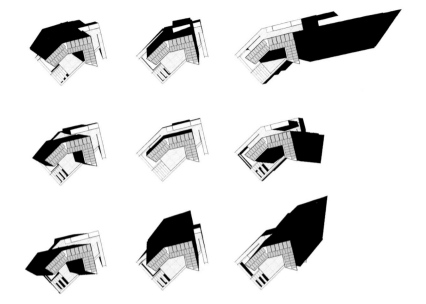

The asymmetry of the house's spatial organization recognizes the fluidity and specificity of life forms, climatic conditions, and natural environments; it is a direct response to the sun's changing position over the course of the day as well as the occupant's variable patterns of inhabitation. Unlike those earlier machines for living in, which were intent on neutralizing, universalizing, and idealizing the specificity of their environs (as was evident in their tendency to emulate bound orthogonal and/or symmetrical organizations), the bent tube of Refract House acts as a flexible spatial and material modulator that efficiently mediates between continuously changing internal activities and external environmental conditions. The material surfaces, spaces, and technologies of the building selectively capture and control, but also subtly adjust and adapt to, the shifting movements of light and thermal energy, moisture and water flow, while simultaneously attempting to maximize the absorption and transformation of energy derived from the unlimited power of the sun. The configuration and southerly orientation of the occupiable spaces of the house and the wide openings, glazed endcaps, and operable clerestories that perforate its exterior skin maximize the admittance of high-quality sunlight and ambient daylighting. Thus they almost eliminate the need for electrical lighting during the day while facilitating natural ventilation and amplifying the connection between interior and exterior. These strategies, in combination with the compactness and efficiency of the architecture's spatial organization, layered ventilated cladding, movable shading systems, interior LED lighting, and

ABOVE
Seasonal and diurnal
shadow study diagram

OPPOSITE
Possible modular
aggregation strategies

exterior self-contained solar-powered LED fixtures, further contribute to minimizing the electric energy load of the house and its subsequent carbon footprint.

Refraction, the phenomenon in which the course of an energy wave is altered when it passes from one medium to another, is manifest in the attitude of the house toward its environs. This "attitude" is one of responsive engagement and flexible modulation, altering and transforming the continuous flows of energy circulating within and through the house. In our contemporary digital milieu, flexible modulation is not limited to the automated movements of mechanical and material systems, but also incorporates instrumentation such as environmental, flow, and pressure sensors, weather monitoring systems, and energy and water consumption tracking devices to enable this living machine to be digitally responsive to environmental changes in real time, and to be calibrated to the needs and desires of its inhabitants. The integration of embedded tracking and control systems, as well as interactive computer technologies that enable this information to be readily accessed via an iPhone application specifically designed for the remote monitoring of the house's environmental performance, furthers this endeavor. It is a "smart house"—seemingly aware of its own artificial metabolism and environmental responsiveness— and it draws its inhabitants into this feedback loop to increase their environmental intelligence and ensure their active, responsive participation in modulating their own consumptive habits. Interactive embedded technologies have thereby made our spaces, systems, and materials seemingly more intelligent, expanding the use value of our designed objects by investing their surfaces and material sensibilities with new performative properties.

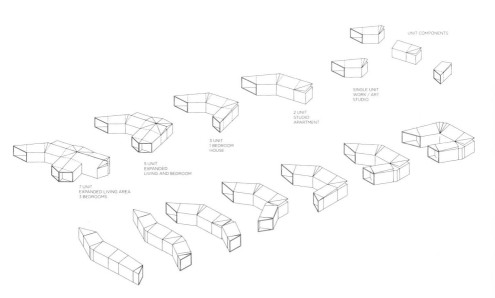

UNIT COMPONENTS

SINGLE UNIT
WORK / ART
STUDIO

2 UNIT
STUDIO
APARTMENT

3 UNIT
1 BEDROOM
HOUSE

5 UNIT
EXPANDED
LIVING AND BEDROOM

7 UNIT
EXPANDED LIVING AREA
3 BEDROOMS

The material approach to Refract House, perhaps situated at the opposite end of this high-tech/low-tech spectrum, redefines ecological responsibility in other terms that are as critical to the concept of environmental performance as the systems previously described. Within this context, the house's environmental responsiveness is equally a measure of its capacity to recycle and reuse the secondary byproducts—essentially the waste—of cultural production, while simultaneously limiting its use of natural materials to those that can be sustainably harvested and regenerated. The intention of this strategy, which focuses on the surplus waste products of our industrialized, consumer-oriented society, consciously attempts to invert the nature-culture continuum by generating new matter from the refuse of disused cultural artifacts. The California redwood siding that forms the house's exterior rainscreen is reclaimed from local fire-damaged stock; the elm flooring and decking is recycled from trees that died of Dutch Elm disease; and the open-web bamboo I-joists and interior finishes are derived from sustainably harvested wood and regenerative materials. Given that trash is currently our largest renewable resource, its repotentialization in Refract House extends its usable life while enabling a set of "post-acculturated" materials to emerge as new products for the construction industry. Billboards discarded after their limited advertising life are thus salvaged and used as the exterior wall waterproofing membrane that wraps the house, and recycled denim and biodegradable soybean-based insulation provide its thermal insulation. Even the interior objects, such as the lighting fixture

ABOVE
Straw light fixture designed by Dave Meeker

BELOW
Weather barrier made from recycled advertising banner

made from disposable straws and the ceramics and glasses from recycled wine bottles, were designed with the intent of transforming our attitude toward cultural production. If steel, concrete, and glass were the new homogeneous industrial materials that signified modernity in the first half of the 20th century, and plastics represented the utopian future in the 1960s, one of our most important raw materials for design in the upcoming decades will be trash.

Embracing cultural continuity while also radically breaking from previous historical paradigms, Refract House is one of a number of contemporary architectural artifacts that emerged through the Solar Decathlon competition that might be imagined to constitute a new set of flexible and biotically integrated machines for living in. These millennial dwelling machines represent an entirely new attitude toward materiality that undermines the "truths" associated with the authenticity of modern materials while blurring earlier distinctions between natural and industrial archetypes through the use of recycled technological products (secondary rather than originary cultural products) and biodegradable and regenerative (rather than exhaustible) natural materials.

These new machines for living in also establish a definition of programmed occupation that goes beyond the limited framework of modern utilitarian functionalism, providing a transformed understanding of environmental efficiency and performance. This new understanding exceeds previous aspirations toward universally controlled, artificial environments fueled by limited natural resources by enabling the flexible modulation of one's own domestic environs using passive environmental strategies in combination with active systems that are powered by harvesting alternative renewable energy sources. If historically the machine was imagined to be the antithesis of nature, as evident in both the American model of the machine in the garden and the European model of the garden embedded within the machine (so to speak), our future imaginary can no longer maintain this oppositional dialectic. We must instead search for new materials and systems that are part of a larger enviro-technological continuum—a blending of nature and culture that supports the making of new living machines, and machines for living in, that are simultaneously innovative, adaptive, and sustainable.

OTES   1. Buckminster Fuller, *Designing a New Industry* (Wichita, Kansas: Fuller Research Institute, 1945.

2. The term "X-urbanism" is used by the architect Mario Gandelsonas to refer to "a contemporary restructuring of the American city where the 'formless' in plan seems to dominate." Gandelsonas refers to a condition where dispersal, rather than density, is the rule, and where the American city, defined more by anti-urban devices such as the highway and a scattered fabric, are essentially characterized as x-urban. See Mario Gandelsonas, *X-Urbanism: Architecture and the American City* (New York: Princeton Architectural Press, 1999): 2–4.

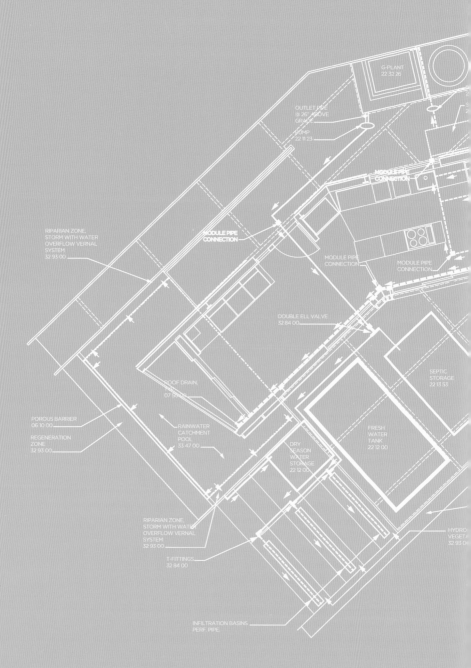

RIPARIAN ZONE,
STORM WITH WATER
OVERFLOW VERNAL
SYSTEM
32 93 00

G-PLANT
22 32 26

OUTLET PIPE
@ 26" ABOVE
GRADE
SUMP
22 11 23

MODULE PIPE
CONNECTION

MODULE PIPE
CONNECTION

MODULE PIPE
CONNECTION

MODULE PIPE
CONNECTION

DOUBLE ELL VALVE
32 84 00

SEPTIC
STORAGE
22 13 53

ROOF DRAIN
PIPE
07 55 00

POROUS BARRIER
06 10 00

RAINWATER
CATCHMENT
POOL
33 47 00

FRESH
WATER
TANK
22 12 00

REGENERATION
ZONE
32 93 00

DRY
SEASON
WATER
STORAGE
22 12 00

RIPARIAN ZONE,
STORM WITH WATER
OVERFLOW VERNAL
SYSTEM
32 93 00

HYDRO-
VEGETA
32 93 0

T-FITTINGS
32 84 00

INFILTRATION BASINS
PERF. PIPE

A1   WETLAND AND INFILTRATION SYSTEM PLAN (WASHINGTON D.C.)

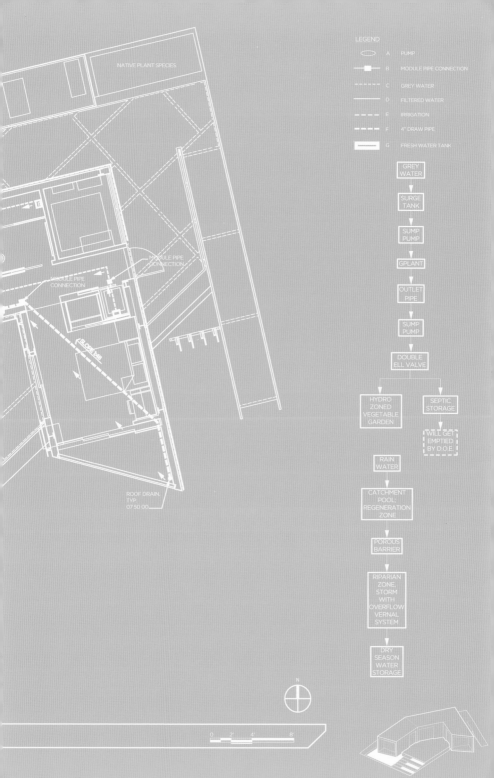

LEGEND

A PUMP
B MODULE PIPE CONNECTION
C GREY WATER
D FILTERED WATER
E IRRIGATION
F 4" DRAW PIPE
G FRESH WATER TANK

NATIVE PLANT SPECIES

MODULE PIPE CONNECTION

MODULE PIPE CONNECTION

ROOF DRAIN,
TYP
07 50 00

GREY WATER

SURGE TANK

SUMP PUMP

G PLANT

OUTLET PIPE

SUMP PUMP

DOUBLE ELL VALVE

HYDRO ZONED VEGETABLE GARDEN

SEPTIC STORAGE

WILL GET EMPTIED BY D.O.E.

RAIN WATER

CATCHMENT POOL; REGENERATION ZONE

POROUS BARRIER

RIPARIAN ZONE, STORM WITH OVERFLOW VERNAL SYSTEM

DRY SEASON WATER STORAGE

N

0 2' 4' 8'

NATIVE PLANT SCHEDULE

MARK	COMMUNITIES	SCIENTIFIC NAME	COMMON NAME	DESCRIPTION	NOTES
A	VALLEY GRASSLAND, FOOTHILL WOODLAND	Thysanocarpus radians	SHOWY FRINGE POD	TINY WHITE FLOWERS WITH WHEEL-SHAPED SEED PODS. EARLY SPRING.	
B	CALIFORNIA EXCEPT SIERRA NEVADAS & DESERT	Chlorogalum pomeridianum	SOAPROOT	FRAGRANT, 6 PETALED WHITE FLOWERS. NATIVE LILY. EDIBLE INNER CORE, USABLE AS FIELD SOAP.	
C	COASTAL, WOODLANDS	Eremocarpus setigerus	TURKEY MULLIEN	WEED-LIKE LOOKING PLANT, TOXIC LEAVES. EDIBLE SEEDS, FAVORS DISTURBED AREAS.	
D	FRESH-WATER WETLANDS, RIPARIAN	Bidens cernua	NODDING BEGGARTICK	GRASSY PLANT WITH SMALL YELLOW FLOWERS AND COARSE PURPLE SEEDS. SPRING, SUMMER, FALL.	
E	FOREST, WOODLANDS, CHAPARRAL, WETLANDS	Rumex salicifolius	WILLOW DOCK	MINUTE CLUSTERED GREEN FLOWERS. SUMMER.	
F	WOODLANDS, SALT MARSH, WETLANDS, RIPARIAN	Sidalcea calycosa	POINT REYES CHECKERBLOOM	BLOOMS ALONGSIDE WHITE-TIPPED CLOVER AT EDGES OF VERNAL POOLS. EARLY SPRING.	
G	FOREST, WOODLANDS, CHAP-ARRAL, WETLANDS, RIPARIAN	Trifolium wormskioldii	WHITE-TIPPED CLOVER	PURPLE FLOWER, WHITE TIPS. SWEET NECTAR. HONEY PRODUCED IS BEST TASTING OF ALL. EARLY SPRING.	
H	WETLAND, RIPARIAN	Eleocharis macrostachya	PALE SPIKERUSH	SHRUB WITH MINUTE CLUSTERED BROWN FLOWERS. SUMMER.	
I	WETLANDS, RIPARIAN	Downingia ornatissima var. ornatissima	FOLDED CALICO-FLOWER	ALSO KNOWN AS 'SKYBLUES', FLOWERS APPEAR IN MASS SYNCHRONY LIKE SKY REFLECTED BY WATER.	
J	FRESHWATER WETLANDS, RIPARIAN	Typha angustifolia	NARROW-LEAVED CATTAIL	NAKED STALK, BETWEEN STAMINATE AND PISTALLATE. SUMMER.	
K	FORESTS, CHAPARRAL, GRASS-LANDS, WETLANDS, RIPARIAN	Deschampsia elongata	SLENDER HAIRGRASS	FIRE RESISTANT. GRASS SPIKELET. FAST GROWING.	
L	FOREST, SAGEBRUSH, GRASS-LAND, WETLAND, RIPARIAN	Alisma plantago-aquatica	WATER PLANTAIN	FOUND IN STREAMBANKS, WHITE FLOWERS WITH YELLOW FRUIT. SPRING, FALL.	
M	SAGEBRUSH, FORESTS, WET-LAND, RIPARIAN	Navarretia leucocephala	WHITE NAVARRETIA	MINUTE PLANT WITH WHITE FLOWERS, ENDEMIC TO VERNAL POOLS OF CENTRAL VALLEY. SPRING.	
N	GRASSLANDS, EVERGREEN FOREST, WETLAND, RIPARIAN	Trifolium depauperatum var. depauperatum	DWARF SACK CLOVER	INDIVIDUAL FLOWERS INFLATE, RESEMBLING SMALL SACKS. HIGHLY NUTRITIOUS.	
O	FOOTHILL WOODLAND, GRASS-LAND, RIPARIAN	Ranunculus bonariensis var. trisepalus	VERNAL POOL BUTTERCUP	GERMINATES EARLY. WHEN POOL IS FULL OF WATER IT PRODUCES LEAVES WITH LONG STEMS, TINY PETALS.	
P	WETLAND, RIPARIAN	Lasthenia fremontii	VERNAL POOL GOLDFIELD	PRODUCES LARGE QUANTITIES OF NUTRITIOUS SEEDS. POLLINATED BY SOLITARY BEES. LATE SPRING.	
Q	WETLANDS, RIPARIAN	Castilleja campestris ssp. Campestris	FIELD OWL'S CLOVER	PRODUCES OWN NUTRITION THROUGH PHOTOSYNTHE-SIS, UNLIKE OTHER OWL'S CLOVER SPECIES.	
R	ASSOCIATED WITH WETLANDS, RIPARIAN	Psilocarphus brevissimus var. brevissimus	WOOLLY MARBLES	IN LATE SEASON, BRACTS ENCLOSE THE FRUITS. EARLY SUMMER.	
S	FORESTS, WOODLAND, GRASS-LANDS, WETLANDS, RIPARIAN	Clematis ligusticifolia var. California	ROPEVINE	CLIMBING, MULTI-STEMMED, GREEN VINE WITH WHITE FLOWERS AND WHITE FRUIT. SPRING, SUMMER.	
T	GRASSLANDS	Carex praegracilis	FIELD SEDGE	LONG NARROW-LEAVED GRASS, LIKE A TUFTED MEADOW. LATE SPRING.	
U	FOREST, WOODLAND, CHAPAR-RAL, GRASSLAND, WETLAND	Cornus glabrata	BROWN DOGWOOD	ESTABLISHES QUICKLY IN WELL-WATERED HABITATS. DECIDUOUS, SMOOTH FOLIAGE.	

(A) (B) (C) (D) (E) (F) (G) (H) (I) (J) (K)

(L) (M) (N) (O) (P) (Q) (R) (S) (T) (U)

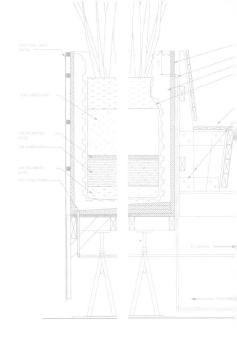

MICRO-ECOSYSTEMS AND ENERGY LOOPS
NATALY GATTEGNO

Refract House could be described quite simply as a sophisticated, highly calibrated, finely tuned home environment: comfortable, insular, small, and controlled. But it is far from a closed, introverted system. Rather, it is tapped into a far larger feedback loop of systems and energies that expand beyond its footprint. From the daylighting systems used to control interior light levels to the HVAC systems that control air quality and temperature, the house is constantly negotiating inputs from its environment, then balancing and redistributing them internally. Refract House, though small in size, is expansive relative to the territory to which it connects, accessing larger inputs of solar energy and orientation, light, heat, ventilation, et cetera. Akin to a micro-ecosystem, it exists somewhere between these energy fields, between internal "comfort zone" requirements and external environmental pressures. This apparent conflict yields a number of challenging and provocative questions: What are the implications of scale in a habitat that responds to multiple environmental inputs? How does energy (solar, thermal, and otherwise) become a design tool? Does the building

envelope become the sole interface for these feedback loops between building and environment? Ultimately, does scale matter?

ABOVE
paraSOL: Daylighting analysis

BELOW
paraSOL: annual sun path diagram

OPPOSITE
paraSOL: annual shadow study and seasonal solar exposure study

Ecosystems in ecology are described as networks of agents that self-organize into complex hierarchies of patterns and processes. The "system" in "ecosystem" implies the importance of interaction between multiple parts.[1] The ecology of ecosystems studies the structure and function of entire systems of agents, whether they are microbes, plants, animals, or buildings, in relation to their abiotic environment.[2] Distinctly different from the evaluative term "environmental," ecosystem ecology describes the behavioral logics of the system: inputs and triggers as opposed to outputs and effects.

The architect Helene Furjan describes an ecosystemic design process as concerned less with an architecture of the object, and more with the management of external environmental influences and internal programmatic energies.[3] Energy management becomes the regulator and designer of these relationships. The design firm AMID.Cero 9 calls the materialization of these energies "energy forms." Energy forms are distinctly different from postwar investigations into material optimization and efficiency. Buckminster Fuller and Frei Otto's visionary explorations of the relationship between energy and form were guided by an interest in material minimization and efficiency rather than material exchange. Exchange and feedback, however, characterize architectural systems that participate in reciprocal relationships with their environments. They privilege exchange over optimization in the determination of the relationship between energy and form. The result is, according to AMID.Cero 9, "a dynamic vision, with systems

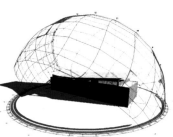

regulated by processes of energy exchange, with exteriors that dissipate, consume and capture energy: complex organizations defined to manage energy through their formal characteristics, technical devices and material definition."[4]

The building is thus no longer conceived as a fixed entity determined by a singular energy type or influence. It is a highly complex ecosystem of multiple energies and influences that are in constant exchange with the environment in which they are situated. These energies have a distinctly nonvisual presence, although their influences do impact form. The invisibility of these energies adds to the elusiveness of this design methodology, which is at once precise and measured, yet ephemeral and invisible. The architect Philippe Rahm writes about the "slippage of the real from the visible towards the invisible . . . a shift of architecture towards the microscopic and atmospheric, the biological and the meteorological."[5] Architecture shifts toward invisible influences (and ultimately, according to Rahm, becomes invisible itself), stretching between the infinitely small and the infinitely large, the scale of the body and the scale of weather systems. In response to the dissolution of built form, new representational systems need to be developed to measure and quantify both the invisible forces applied to the architectural form and the visible outcome of those interactions. Further, these representational systems need to span multiple scales of influence, from weather patterns to temperature gradients and ergonomic body comfort.

Scale, under these terms, is consequently of no importance, and subservient to the interactions between all the parts. Ecosystems describe systems that span scales and are able to address hyper local and global realms through their behavioral logics. They are constantly confronted with a range of environmental fluctuations that vary constantly in magnitude and force. The scale of ecological dynamics can therefore operate as a closed system with respect to local site variables, while at the same time remain open with regard to broader systemic influences that change over time.

Although this publication focuses on Refract House and its building performance at the level of the 2009 Solar Decathlon competition, it touches on multiple overlapping conditions of energy exchange that go beyond the building's walls and engage various scales of operation. Refract House explores the many interactions that take place between the house and its broader ecosystemic environment. These larger loops and cycles are ar-

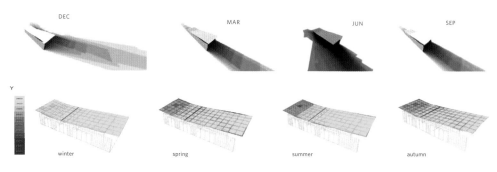

ticulated elsewhere in these pages by Kate Simonen, who describes the extremely broad impact of the house when seen through the lens of a carbon neutral design process. Peter Anderson's discussion of the prefabricated components of the house expands to consider larger infrastructural scales of operation, while Matt Hutchinson and Oblio Jenkins's description of material cycles and assembly processes zooms even further into the material scale. Tim Hight's description of the engineering systems, though extremely focused on the scale of the house and its inner workings, can be considered the hinge point where the expansive environmental energies intersect with the building components. Ila Berman's essay makes the larger conceptual loop back out to machinic ecosystems, while Andrew Kudless's presentation of the design process describes the collaborative loops necessary between disciplines and processes.

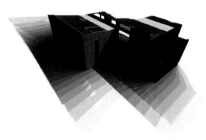

These ecosystemic interactions are not relegated to the boundary of inside and outside and are not solely limited to explorations of building skin. Although the term "boundary" usually describes a physical condition of separation, for example a site of heat transfer, the concept could be expanded to include the larger zone of heat exchange. In Refract House, conventional notions of boundary, skin, and envelope are considered thick zones—extended to include the entire building in physical terms, and thickened even further to include the broader tentacles of energy exchange and interaction that take place with the larger ecology of the site and systems. The boundary between building and environment merges into one thick and continuous ecosystem described by complex energy gradients that fluctuate and evolve over time. The constant recalibration and modulation of the architectural enclosure describes the microecosystem of Refract House. Though fixed in terms of its footprint, the building is constantly modulated to address and respond to environmental influences.

Refract House is simultaneously looped into its surrounding environment and the larger web of ecosystems of production, consumption, assembly, and fabrication, while at the same time literally connected to the techno-logical machinery needed to sustain the architectural comfort zone. By understanding the expansive web of influences interacting with the house, it becomes possible to understand the larger and more complex inter-relationships between this small building and its expanded environment. AMID.Cero 9 calls these interrelationships the "biotechnosocial" realm of architecture, in which everything produced—that is, architecture—can be defined as a manifestation of interactions among humans, nature, and technological objects.[6] The microecology of Refract House is therefore far from "micro" in its impact on design and form.

NOTES   1. For a detailed discussion of this topic, see Ferenc Jordán and István Scheuring, "Network Ecology: Topological Constraints on Ecosystem Dynamics," *Physics of Life Reviews* no. 1 (2004): 139–72.

2. Kevin Kelly, *Out of Control: The New Biology of Machines, Social Systems, and the Economic World* (Cambridge: Addison Wesley, 1994): 69–91.

3. Helene Furjan, "Eco-logics" in *Softspace: From a Representation of Form to a Simulation of Space*, eds. Sean Lally and Jessica Young (London and New York: Routledge, 2007): 115.

4. Cristina Díaz Moreno and Efrén García Grinda, "Energy Forms" in *Energies: New Material Boundaries: Architectural Design*, ed. Sean Lally (London: Wiley, 2009): 83.

5. Philippe Rahm, "Meteorological Architecture" in *Energies*, 32.

6. Moreno and Grinda, "Energy Forms," 83.

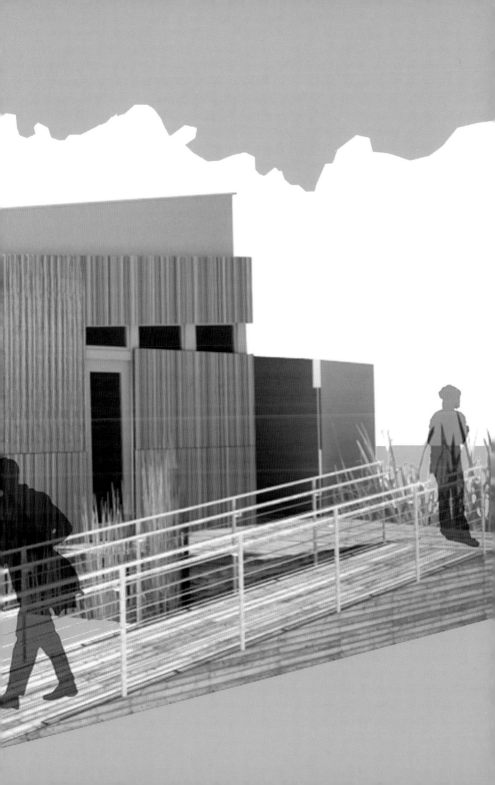

DESIGN
STRATEGIES

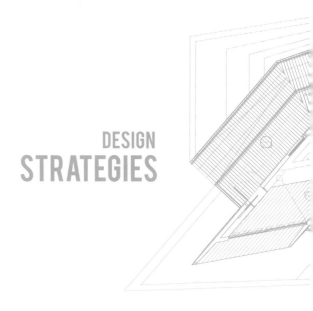

BUILDING LIGHT
ANDREW KUDLESS

During the schematic design process of Refract House, our task was to fuse the most advanced engineering knowledge with forward-thinking architectural strategies and innovative design. At the outset we had two main objectives. First, the teams from CCA and Santa Clara University needed to form a working relationship that would sustain the project over a two-year period. Each team had much to learn from the other, and the sooner we could collaboratively resolve the essential issues of the design, the more time we would have for the difficult process of developing and building a full-scale project. As an experienced engineering team, the faculty and students at SCU were able to educate us about the competition as well as the fundamental, real-world engineering problems inherent in the competition brief. Likewise, as architects and designers, one of the main tasks for the CCA faculty and students was to educate the SCU team about the architectural process and expose them to innovative design strategies. In the early design phase, a critical dialogue evolved

enabling the gradual emergence of a collective design intent. Through these conversations it was determined that the house should reflect the climate and lifestyle of California by connecting its inhabitants with their environment. The phrase "Building Light" became the working title of the schematic design studios, as the dual meaning of the word "light" (as an energy wavelength and as a measure of weight) spoke to our intent to have a light environmental footprint. Our goal was to build lightly on the landscape in terms of energy and materials, and also spatial engagement of the ground.

The second objective of these initial studios was to create a schematic design that satisfied this intent and had the conceptual strength to be further developed in later studios, which would focus on design development and detailing, the production of construction documents and technical specifications, and the final fabrication of the built project on the National Mall in Washington DC. All architectural design projects must negotiate between conceptual design intent and the realities of cost, materials, and fabrication. Ideally, this process is one of iterative refinement whereby the original concept becomes richer and more detailed as the process progresses. This process often breaks down if the original concept

is unclear or uninspiring, as it will not have the power to help drive design decisions later on. This issue was even more important for our team, since the schematic design would be handed over to different groups of students involved in subsequent phases of the project.

The first studio was divided into three phases that involved individual as well as collaborative research and design. The initial research phase focused on four areas that were essential to understanding the design brief:

Schematic Design Prototypes

ABOVE
Response House: front view

BELOW
Response House: view along Washington Mall

OPPOSITE TOP
Response House: aggregation of component units

OPPOSITE BELOW
Response House: modular breakdown and transportation diagram

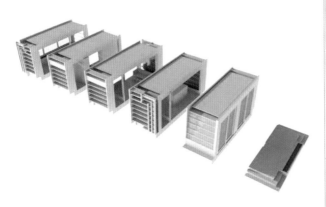

analysis of previous submissions to the competition, architectural prefabrication, contemporary compact residential design, and sustainable systems and materials. Through an analysis of these four areas, the students began to understand the difficult task in front of them. Not only were they being challenged to design something that dozens of teams before them had already tried, but they were also being asked to innovate in three critically important emerging areas of design. This analysis provided a framework for understanding the central design problems of the competition and enabled the studio to innovate within this framework. For example, several students were responsible for drawing parti diagrams of all the past Solar Decathlon projects, and it became clear that nearly all of them fell into one of a handful of formal typologies: long single bar, long bar with appendages, shifted double bar, or multiple parallel bars. When these typologies were cross-referenced with the scores the entries had earned in the competition, it was clear that projects that minimized the number of prefabricated modules while also producing a clear mechanical/bathroom/kitchen core did better in the Decathlon events. Furthermore, it also became clear that at

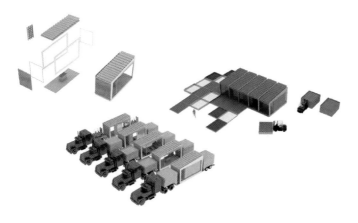

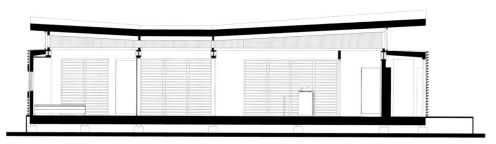

the scale of compact residential design, the use of a clear and simple formal strategy was advantageous, as more complex spatial layouts tended to make the interior spaces feel too compact and fragmented.

The second phase of the studio was framed as a competition among all 16 students. They used the knowledge gained in the first phase to propose various design strategies that addressed the issues of prefabrication, sustainable material systems research, and the lessons learned generally from their investigation of both contemporary compact residential design and specifically from the successes and failures of previous Solar Decathlon

entries. Each student proposed not only a design solution for the single-family house as per the competition brief, but also an urban design strategy for how the units might aggregate into larger assemblages forming sustainable urban communities. Although this latter was not part of the original brief from the United States Department of Energy, we felt that designing projects that considered their larger urban context was appropriate and responsible.

From this group of 16 projects, four were selected to be further developed based on a range of criteria that included the potential success of their sustainable design strategies, their innovation, and their capacity to be prefabricated, transported, and reassembled on site. One of the issues raised was the construction time required for the use of flat-pack

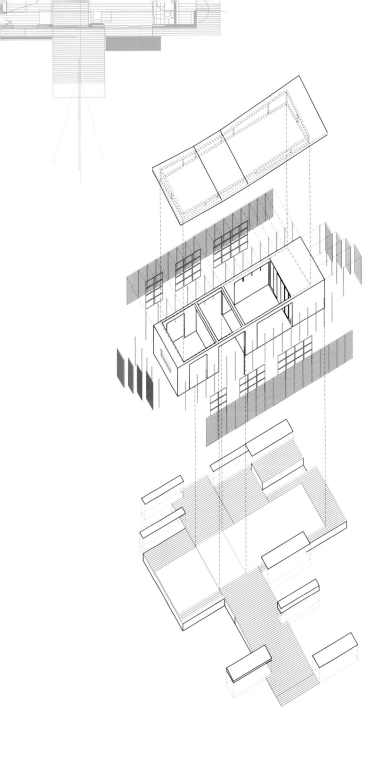

systems that were included in some of the early design proposals. Although highly sustainable due to the minimization of space required during transport, flat-pack systems would have required too much time for on-site assembly given the constraints of the competition. Similarly, although many of the projects proposed very innovative energy generation and storage systems, some of these were unproven and potentially too expensive. Although all of the proposals were interesting, the realities of budget and schedule superseded a desire to explore radically experimental material or energy generation systems. Lastly, we felt that the final four should constitute a range of different formal design solutions. They ended up representing the following typologies: single bar, shifted double bar, multiple parallel bar, and a new typology we named the bent bar.

These four projects were then developed over the final four weeks of the studio by teams comprised of the original designer plus three other students.

RESPONSE HOUSE Response House, the first of the final four, was an elegant design solution based on five parallel, prefabricated modules. Based on a "box within a box" concept, the project used multiple skins to modulate light, air, and program. Through a combination of movable shading devices and sliding doors, the house could be quickly reconfigured for different temperatures and programs. At its most open, nearly all of the house's walls would be either slid or folded away, leaving a large open space spanning the covered deck, bedroom, and living areas. At its most closed, the space would be subdivided into five smaller rooms that could be heated or cooled individually, as needed, based on local conditions and programmatic needs. This strategy was based on traditional Japanese residential design whereby walls slide open in summer to allow cross-ventilation and slide closed in winter to trap heat in specific rooms. In addition, the team proposed an efficient and well-designed landscape scheme that included hard, soft, and water modular components. The louvered skin formed a minimal yet complex texture across the facade that provided both privacy and shade for the occupants.

paraSOL was a simple formal solution that was complex in its ability to reconfigure to changing weather and program. Designed as a singular module, the project probably had one of the simplest construction PARASOL sequences of the final four. The straightforward, linear plan could be used as one long space or subdivided into three smaller spaces that included a covered exterior space. Like Response House, the facade featured a complex series of louvers that could be reconfigured in a variety of ways to produce many different performances with respect to light, air, and privacy. The project was capped with a butterfly roof that opened up at either end of the bar to allow more light and air to enter the space as well as to produce a feeling of compression at the covered deck area in the center. A

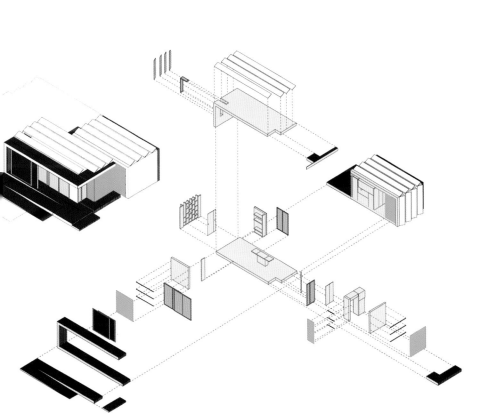

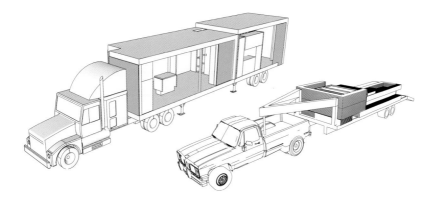

long deck, connecting the public exterior space to a private garden along the north side, bisected the project.

Cap House used a shifted double-bar typology that attempted to minimize the required number of transportation trucks while maximizing the feeling of a large, open interior space. This project proposed several innovative material strategies, for instance reusing waste from the agricultural and construction industries to produce components for the house: composite waste-straw fiberboard for the walls and reclaimed lumber for the decking. The project took advantage of ongoing research projects at SCU, such as the use of compressed straw to make fiberboard. The formal simplicity of the double C-shaped bars integrated the project into the landscape. The floor of the front bar gradually transitioned from the reclaimed wood decking into a series of planted areas. The project also engaged the modular capacity of the design to propose large aggregates that could support larger single-family and multiple-family units.

ABOVE
Cap House: truck loading diagram

BELOW
Cap House: component assembly sequence

OPPOSITE
Cap House: interior views

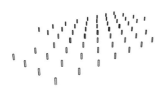

Small piles are erected to support the house components.

The two main components are set in place with a crane; both components' moment frames are attached.

Refract House broke away from the established prefabricated formal typologies. Rather than working with variations on single or parallel bars, it joined three modules end-to-end and bent them around a central court-

yard. This simple but innovative solution aligned best with the studio's overall objective of connecting indoor and outdoor living—an opportunity afforded by the temperate California climate and lifestyle. All rooms of the house had direct connections to the courtyard, making the exterior the most important "room" in the project. Although this volume of the house was similar to that of the other three, it appeared much bigger because of the courtyard space. Finally, the use of cantilevers to project the ends of the house out over the landscape evoked a sense of weightlessness; the house seemed to hover over the rainwater collection pond and other garden features. The cantilevers also formally communicated the desire to "build lightly" on the landscape, an idea that was addressed mechani-

cally and materially as well through the use of a full-roof solar array and various recycled building components such as shredded-denim insulation.

Deck and sunscreen devices are attached to main building components.

Ramps and solar panels are attached.

 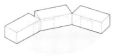 

An external board of experts, including local architects and engineers, reviewed the four projects and made the final decision that Refract House would be the one developed further for the competition. The jurors commented that any of the four projects could easily have moved on to be developed, but that Refract House presented the most innovative of the four solutions. As a school of architecture, it is important that we continuously push the boundaries of design in order to advance our discipline. This support of experimentation brings with it many risks, of course, and we were well aware that Refract House, due to its geometry, would present critical challenges as we moved forward.

After Refract House was selected, a three-week summer studio rapidly began work on refining the design **REFRACT HOUSE** for our Design Development submission to the Department of Energy. Two important changes occurred during this time that helped clarify the overall design concept. The first was a refinement of the exterior decking and interior form to reinforce the layering of garden, decking, house, and built-ins; the garden and decking on the exterior and a series of benches, counters, and other built-in furniture on the interior became more clearly a series of parallel bands of program that complemented the strong formal simplicity of the bent-tube massing. The second change was the development of a wood skin that helped focus the form on the two large openings at each end of the bent tube.

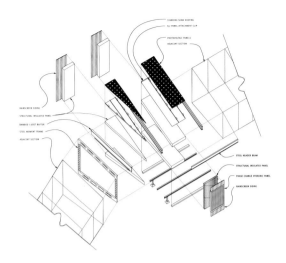

Numerous other important developments were devised during later studios, but the work of the early design team was indispensable in establishing the strong conceptual framework and design parameters. In the end, Refract House was a successful experiment in the possibilities of creative design thinking and collaboration.

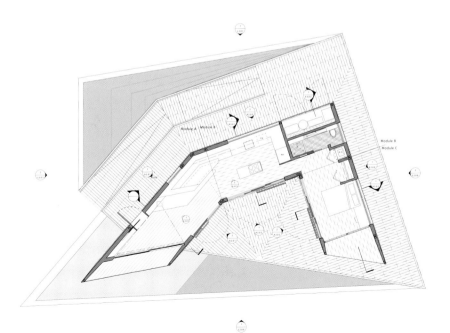

PARASOL

CAP HOUSE

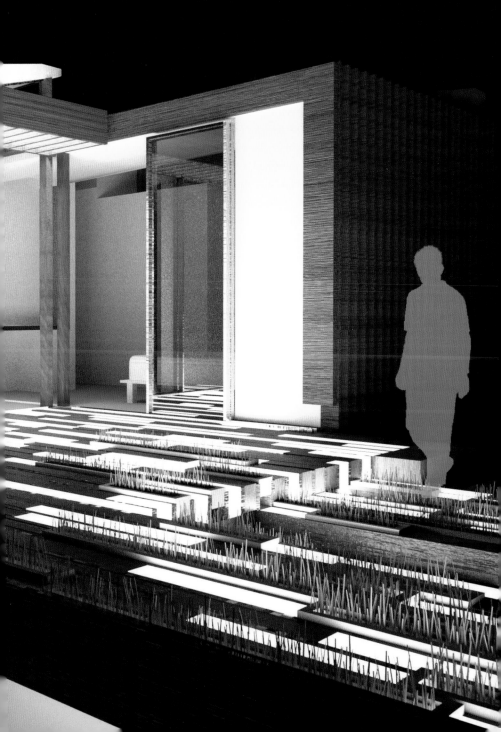

REFRACT HOUSE

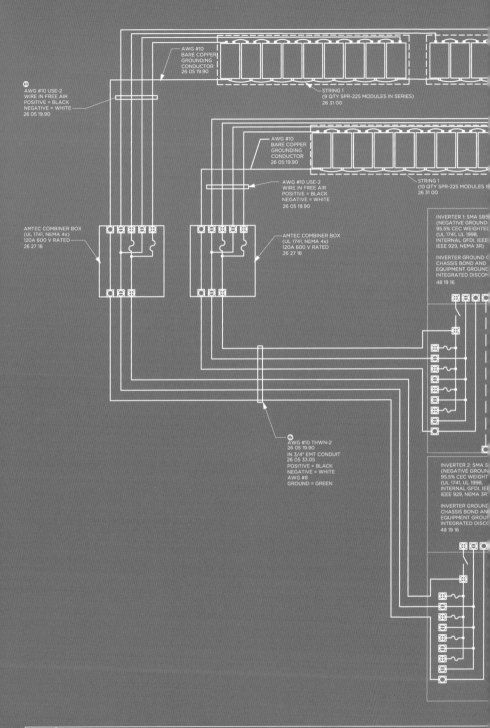

AWG #10
BARE COPPER
GROUNDING
CONDUCTOR
26 05 19.90

AWG #10 USE-2
WIRE IN FREE AIR
POSITIVE = BLACK
NEGATIVE = WHITE
26 05 19.90

STRING 1
(9 QTY SPR-225 MODULES IN SERIES)
26 31 00

AWG #10
BARE COPPER
GROUNDING
CONDUCTOR
26 05 19.90

AWG #10 USE-2
WIRE IN FREE AIR
POSITIVE = BLACK
NEGATIVE = WHITE
26 05 19.90

STRING 1
(10 QTY SPR-225 MODULES I
26 31 00

AMTEC COMBINER BOX
(UL 1741, NEMA 4x)
120A 600 V RATED
26 27 16

AMTEC COMBINER BOX
(UL 1741, NEMA 4x)
120A 600 V RATED
26 27 16

INVERTER 1: SMA SB5
(NEGATIVE GROUND)
95.5% CEC WEIGHTED
(UL 1741, UL 1998,
INTERNAL GFDI, IEEE
IEEE 929, NEMA 3R)

INVERTER GROUND C
CHASSIS BOND AND
EQUIPMENT GROUND
INTEGRATED DISCON
48 19 16

AWG #10 THWN-2
26 05 19.90
IN 3/4" EMT CONDUIT
26 05 33.05
POSITIVE = BLACK
NEGATIVE = WHITE
AWG #8
GROUND = GREEN

INVERTER 2: SMA S
(NEGATIVE GROUN
95.5% CEC WEIGHT
(UL 1741, UL 1998,
INTERNAL GFDI, IE
IEEE 929, NEMA 3R

INVERTER GROUND
CHASSIS BOND AN
EQUIPMENT GROUP
INTEGRATED DISCO
48 19 16

A1	THREE LINE DIAGRAM
	NTS

PR-225 MODULES IN SERIES)

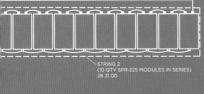

STRING 2
(10 QTY SPR-225 MODULES IN SERIES)
26 31 00

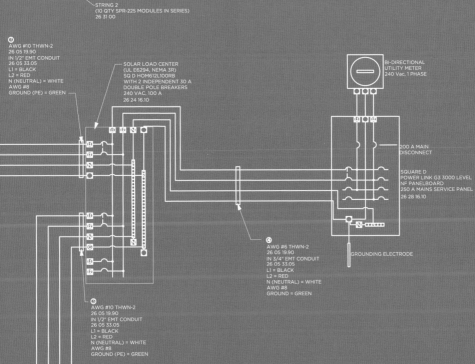

AWG #10 THWN-2
26 05 19.90
IN 1/2" EMT CONDUIT
26 05 33.05
L1 = BLACK
L2 = RED
N (NEUTRAL) = WHITE
AWG #8
GROUND (PE) = GREEN

SOLAR LOAD CENTER
(UL E6294, NEMA 3R)
SQ D HOM612L100RB
WITH 2 INDEPENDENT 30 A
DOUBLE POLE BREAKERS
240 VAC, 100 A
26 24 16.10

BI-DIRECTIONAL
UTILITY METER
240 Vac, 1 PHASE

200 A MAIN
DISCONNECT

SQUARE D
POWER LINK G3 3000 LEVEL
NF PANELBOARD
250 A MAINS SERVICE PANEL
26 28 16.10

AWG #6 THWN-2
26 05 19.90
IN 3/4" EMT CONDUIT
26 05 33.05
L1 = BLACK
L2 = RED
N (NEUTRAL) = WHITE
AWG #8
GROUND = GREEN

GROUNDING ELECTRODE

AWG #10 THWN-2
26 05 19.90
IN 1/2" EMT CONDUIT
26 05 33.05
L1 = BLACK
L2 = RED
N (NEUTRAL) = WHITE
AWG #8
GROUND (PE) = GREEN

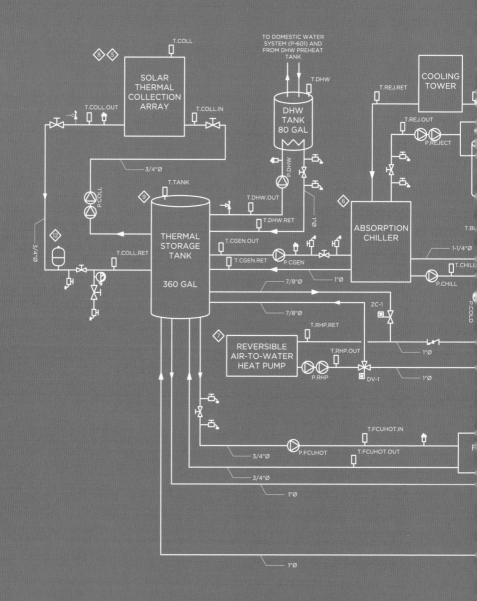

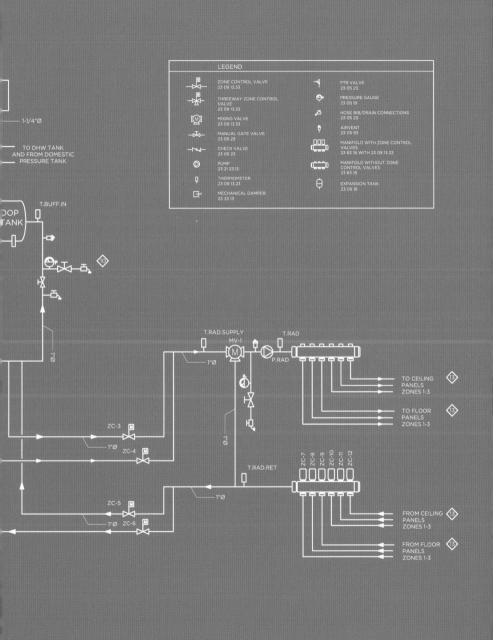

LEGEND

ZONE CONTROL VALVE 23 09 13.33	PTR VALVE 23 05 23
THREEWAY ZONE CONTROL VALVE 23 09 13.33	PRESSURE GAUGE 23 05 19
MIXING VALVE 23 09 13.33	HOSE BIB/DRAIN CONNECTIONS 23 05 23
MANUAL GATE VALVE 23 05 23	AIRVENT 23 05 93
CHECK VALVE 23 05 23	MANIFOLD WITH ZONE CONTROL VALVES 23 83 16 WITH 23 09 13.33
PUMP 23 21 23.13	MANIFOLD WITHOUT ZONE CONTROL VALVES 23 83 16
THERMOMETER 23 09 13.23	EXPANSION TANK 23 05 16
MECHANICAL DAMPER 23 33 13	

1-1/4"Ø

TO DHW TANK
AND FROM DOMESTIC
PRESSURE TANK

OOP
TANK

T.BUFF.IN

Ø-1

T.RAD.SUPPLY
MV-1

T.RAD
P.RAD

1"Ø

TO CEILING
PANELS
ZONES 1-3

TO FLOOR
PANELS
ZONES 1-3

Ø-1

ZC-3

1"Ø ZC-4

ZC-7 ZC-8 ZC-9 ZC-10 ZC-11 ZC-12

T.RAD.RET

1"Ø

ZC-5

1"Ø ZC-6

FROM CEILING
PANELS
ZONES 1-3

FROM FLOOR
PANELS
ZONES 1-3

DDC CONTROL EQUIPMENT

NAME	COUNT	LOCATION	MAKE	MASTER FORMAT CODE
TEMP SENSOR (OUTDOOR)	1	ON ROOF ABOVE MECHROOM	UPONOR	23 09 13.23
TEMP SENSOR (SLAB)	6	IN-FLOOR AT BEGINNING OF RADIANT TUBING RUNS	UPONOR	23 09 13.23
WALL TEMP SENSOR (NO DISPLAY)	3	AS SPECIFIED ON M-101	UPONOR	23 09 13.23
THERMOSTAT (WALL DISPLAY)	1	AS SPECIFIED ON M-101	UPONOR	23 09 13
ROUTER MAIN CONTROLLER	1	IN NETWORK CONTROLS CABINET (M-201)	UPONOR	23 09 00
PRIMARY EQUIPMENT CONTROLLER	1	IN NETWORK CONTROLS CABINET (M-201)	UPONOR	23 09 00
SUPPLY WATER TEMP CONTROLLER	1	IN NETWORK CONTROLS CABINET (M-201)	UPONOR	23 09 00
CONTROL CABINET, 4 POSITION		ON CONTROLS WALL (M-201)	UPONOR	23 09 00
FURNACE/AC CONTROL BOARD	1	ON FCU (M-201)	UPONOR	23 09 00
HRV CONTROL BOARD	1	ON ERV (M-201)	UPONOR	23 09 00
ZONE VALVE AND DAMPER CONTROL BOARD	2	ON HYDRONICS WALL (M-201)	UPONOR	23 09 00
GENERIC I/O CONTROL MODULE	1	IN NETWORK CONTROLS CABINET (M-201)	UPONOR	23 09 00
BOILER RELAY BOX	1	ON HYDRONICS WALL (M-201)	UPONOR	23 09 00
PUMP RELAY BOX	13	ON PUMPS ON HYDRONICS WALL	UPONOR	23 09 00
TRANSFORMER (50 VA)	4	WITH ASSOCIATED EQUIPMENT	UPONOR	23 09 00

A1 | DDC CONTROL EQUIPMENT SCHEDULE
NO SCALE

REGISTER AND VENT SCHEDULE

TYPE	LOCATION	FLOW RATE	MAKE	MODEL	SIZE	MASTER FORMAT CODE
SUPPLY DIFFUSER LINEAR BAR FLOOR TYPE	BEDROOM	75 CFM	TITUS	CT-480	3" X 12"	23 37 13.10
SUPPLY DIFFUSER LINEAR BAR FLOOR TYPE	KITCHEN	75 CFM	TITUS	CT-480	3" X 12"	23 37 13.10
SUPPLY DIFFUSER LINEAR BAR FLOOR TYPE	LIVING ROOM	50 CFM	TITUS	CT-480	3" X 12"	23 37 13.10
SUPPLY DIFFUSER LINEAR BAR FLOOR TYPE	LIVING ROOM	50 CFM	TITUS	CT-480	3" X 12"	23 37 13.10
RETURN GRILLE WALL TYPE	HALLWAY NEAR MECHROOM	250 CFM	TITUS	AEROBLADE GRILL 56-FL	18" X 24"	23 37 13.30
GRAVITY VENT	ROOF EXHAUST	250 CFM	GREENHECK	GRSR-10	10"	23 37 13

D5 | SCHEDULES
NO SCALE

HEAT PUMPS AND CHILLER PLANTS

TYPE	MAKE AND MODEL	POWER	VOLTAGE	WEIGHT	REFRIGERANT TYPE	EFF	ELECTRIC POWER	MASTER FORMAT CODE
REVERSIBLE HEAT PUMP	MULTIAQUA MAC-036	36,000 BTU/HR	208/230 - 60 HZ	310 LBS	R-407C	13.0 EER	3300 W	23 81 43
ABSORPTION CHILLER	SONNENKLIMA SUNINVERSE 10KW	34,100 BTU/HR	230 V - 1 PH 50 HZ	1200 LBS	LIBR AND WATER	0.79 COP	120 W	23 64 13.16
COOLING TOWER	SONNENKLIMA WCT23KW	80,000 BTU/HR	230 V - 1 PH 50 HZ	330 LBS	WATER	N/A	350 W	23 65 13.13

C5 HEAT PUMP AND CHILLER PLANT SCHEDULE
NO SCALE

TANKS

MAKE	FUNCTION	TYPE	SIZE	DIAMETER	HEIGHT OR LENGTH	INSULATION	MASTER FORMAT CODE
NILES	THERMAL STORAGE	PRESSURIZED BUFFER TANK	360 GAL	36"	7'-10"	BLOWN CLOSED-CELL FOAM, R-20	23 71 13.23
SUPERSTOR	DHW	INDIRECT DHW	80 GAL	24"	6'-0"	FACTORY JACKED	22 35 29.16
SUPERSTOR	DHW PREHEAT	INDIRECT DHW	80 GAL	24"	6'-0"	FACTORY JACKETED	22 35 29.16
NILES	CHILLED WATER BUFFER	PRESSURIZED HORIZONTAL BUFFER TANK	130 GAL	2'-0"	7'-6"	BLOWN CLOSED-CELL FOAM, R-15	23 71 16

D3 TANK SCHEDULE
NO SCALE

SOLAR THERMAL COLLECTORS

MAKE	MODEL	TYPE	AREA	DIMENSIONS (GROSS)	EFFICIENCY (ASHRAE)	HEAT LOSS COEFFICIENT (ASHRAE)	MASTER FORMAT CODE
SCHUCO	SCHUCOSOL DG	FLAT PLATE, DOUBLE GLAZED	29 SQ. FT	84.5" X 59.5" X 4.5"	.79	3.9 W/M²K	23 56 13.13

E3 SOLAR THERMAL PANEL SCHEDULE
NO SCALE

MECHANICAL DAMPERS

APPLICATION	MAKE	MODEL	MASTERFORMAT CODE
EXHAUST OPERATION	TITUS	VAV RETROFIT TERMINAL DECV 8"	23 33 13
INTAKE OPERATION	TITUS	VAV RETROFIT TERMINAL DECV 8"	23 33 13

E5 MECHANICAL DAMPER SCHEDULE
NO SCALE

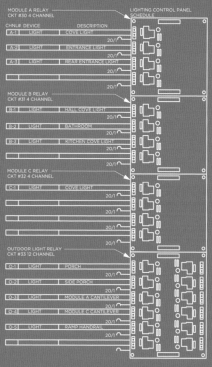
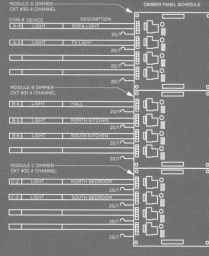

MODULE A RELAY
CKT #30 4 CHANNEL

LIGHTING CONTROL PANEL SCHEDULE

CHNL#	DEVICE	DESCRIPTION
A-1	LIGHT	COVE LIGHT
		20/1
A-2	LIGHT	ENTRANCE LIGHT
		20/1
A-3	LIGHT	REAR ENTRANCE LIGHT
		20/1

MODULE B RELAY
CKT #31 4 CHANNEL

B-1	LIGHT	HALL COVE LIGHT
		20/1
B-2	LIGHT	BATHROOM
		20/1
B-3	LIGHT	KITCHEN COVE LIGHT
		20/1

MODULE C RELAY
CKT #32 4 CHANNEL

C-1	LIGHT	COVE LIGHT
		20/1
		20/1
		20/1

OUTDOOR LIGHT RELAY
CKT #33 12 CHANNEL

O-1	LIGHT	PORCH
		20/1
O-2	LIGHT	SIDE PORCH
		20/1
O-3	LIGHT	MODULE A CANTILEVER
		20/1
O-4	LIGHT	MODULE C CANTILEVER
		20/1
O-5	LIGHT	RAMP HANDRAIL
		20/1

MODULE A DIMMER
CKT #30 4 CHANNEL

DIMMER PANEL SCHEDULE

CHNL#	DEVICE	DESCRIPTION
A-4	LIGHT	SOFA LIGHT
		20/1
A-5	LIGHT	TV LIGHT
		20/1
		20/1
		20/1

MODULE B DIMMER
CKT #31 4 CHANNEL

B-4	LIGHT	HALL
		20/1
B-5	LIGHT	NORTH KITCHEN
		20/1
B-6	LIGHT	SOUTH KITCHEN
		20/1
		20/1

MODULE C DIMMER
CKT #32 4 CHANNEL

C-2	LIGHT	NORTH BEDROOM
		20/1
C-3	LIGHT	SOUTH BEDROOM
		20/1
		20/1
		20/1

20/1 ⌐ DENOTES A 20 AMP / 1 POLE / 120V / 208V / OR 277V RELAY FED FROM BREAKER INSIDE PANELBOARD

20/2 ⌐ DENOTES A 20 AMP / 2 POLE / 208V / OR 480V RELAY FED FROM BREAKER INSIDE PANELBOARD

A1 | LIGHTING RELAY
NO SCALE

PANEL "EXP1"			TYPE: 120/240 VOLT, 1 PHASE, 3W.		LOCATION: VERIFY			MOUNTING: SURFACE		
			MAINS: 100 AMPS M.L.O.							

CKT NO.	SERVING	CIRCUIT LOAD		BRKR.			BRKR.	CIRCUIT LOAD		SERVING	CKT NO.
		ø A	ø B	TRIP			TRIP	ø A	ø B		
1	SMA5000	1440		30/2							2
3			360	↑							4
5	SMA5000	540		30/2							6
7			250	↑							8
9											10
11											12

TOTAL ø A: VA
TOTAL ø B: VA

TOTAL CONNECTED VA

[N] PANEL SHALL BE SQUARE "D"
TYPE "NQOD" WITH GROUND
AND NEUTRAL BUSSES 42 CKT.

*PROVIDE LOCKED ON CKT. BKR.
**PROVIDE ARC FAULT CKT. BKR.

C4 | LOAD CENTER BREAKER
NO SCALE

TECHNOLOGICAL
SYSTEMS

ENGINEERING FOR OPTIMIZED PERFORMANCE
TIM HIGHT

The engineering design of Refract House aspired to seamlessly integrate technology and design without compromising architectural aspirations or habitability. While remaining mindful of the direct measures used in judging the contest, the makers of the house attempted to optimize the building design and systems to perform as efficiently as possible for the house's entire future lifespan, employing technologies and design practices at the forefront of sustainable building.

Refract House is not a typical "green" home, in the sense that solar energy and energy efficiency were not afterthoughts. Rather, both were integral parts of the house's design and engineering. Although SEAMLESS INTEGRATION the process necessitated some negotiation and compromise, the architectural design of the house makes as few concessions as possible in engineering efficiency. Vast, thermally insulated windows allow for unobstructed views of the surrounding landscape, and radiant cooling (a system of

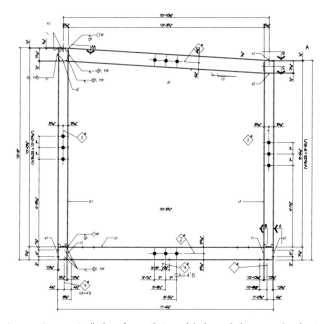

temperature-controlled surfaces that cool indoor air by removing heat through thermal radiation) allows the large glazed entryways to be opened onto the expansive cantilevered deck, even during the summer.

From the exterior, the solar collectors appear as a single roof plane, the redwood siding provides an extra thermal barrier, and the windows balance daylight and thermal demands through advanced glazing and controllable external shades. On the interior, energy monitoring, lighting controls, and environmental controls are subtle and functional, and all of the sophisticated systems that enable the house to run quietly and efficiently are imperceptible.

The house was designed in three modules for easy transportation from California to Washington DC and back. Each module was made using standard wood-frame construction with six-inch-thick walls integrated with steel moment frames.[1] Robust and stiff, it was able to survive transportation with minimal damage and full compliance with flatbed truck size and steering limitations. On site in Washington DC, the three modules were easily assembled in just a few days. This modularity was intended as an overarching design strategy that in future potential iterations of the prototype would enable the basic design of the house to be extended into other, larger configurations as desired.

The house's spatial configuration and external envelope were extensively modeled and analyzed for thermal performance. The results of this modeling and analysis enabled precise calibration of the build- ing design and material choices for optimum efficiency. For example, the highly engineered glazing, which incorporates a "heat mirror" film within a dual-pane window, insulates almost as well as a triple-paned window but with considerably less weight and expense. Sophisticated external shading allows for shade in the summer and passive solar gain in the winter. The house incorporates advanced soybean-based blown insulation in the floor, walls, and ceilings for thermal isolation and infiltration control (with an R value of 24.5)[2] along with aerogel-based thermal bridging prevention for critical building details to ensure that heat and cold aren't transferred across its enclosure. The house features a "cool roof" design with solar panels racked above the roof, and a weather-stopping "skin" on the walls. Both of these allow air to flow, prevent solar gain, and shield the house from the elements for a longer lifespan.

Each system of the house is optimized for efficiency, and sized to meet and exceed all foreseeable demands. The roof solar collector array was modeled to determine the best arrangement and orientation of solar electric panels, to result in peak energy density for our target conditions within the contest limits on building height. Using 48 SunPower 225 panels, it has demonstrated a peak capacity of 10.8 kW. In order to take full advantage of the photovoltaic array, the house is designed for an all-electric approach, including the use of a high-efficiency reversible heat pump for both heating and cooling. All electrical loads are minimized, and circuits and displays are configured to give the user easy knowledge of, access to, and control over all devices. This includes the ability to turn off circuits with so-called "phantom

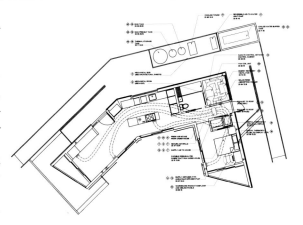

currents" due to standby power for appliances and chargers. These phantom currents can sometimes account for up to 10 percent of a household's total energy consumption.

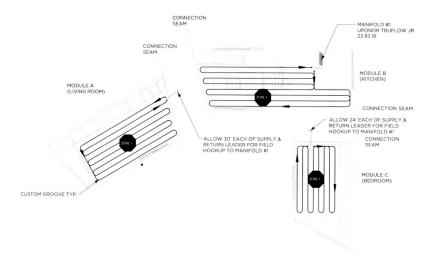

ABOVE
Radiant floor heating/
cooling zones relative to
building modules

The mechanical systems are meticulously designed with the most efficient equipment, using innovative features such as radiant heating and cooling in both floor and ceiling, energy recovery ventilation (ERV), mechanical cooling, and ERV bypass for mild weather. The radiant system both cools and heats the house using water circulating in tubes embedded in panels in the floor and ceiling. It has six different zones, each independently controllable. This allows for sophisticated fine-tuning of the temperature in each of the building modules, for example allowing the sun to heat the kitchen area while the bedroom remains cool. The use of radiant panels for cooling is relatively new, because the control system must be sophisticated enough to monitor and adjust for the dew point, preventing condensation from forming on the ceiling or floor.

The house also incorporates a forced-air ventilation system so fresh air can be distributed throughout, thus accommodating more rapid changes in room temperature. Energy recovery ventilation is used within this system so that normally exhausted energy can be recovered and reused to pre-heat and pre-cool (as well as dehumidify) incoming air. Designing for the future is why radiant cooling was employed, even though the contest metrics did not favor it. It is also why DC boost box technology was pursued until it was absolutely certain it would not be certified in time. (This feature has since been added to the house.) DC boost technology is a wireless monitoring and power optimizing system that enables localized artificial balancing of current flow in a solar panel system as a way to ensure the largest yield possible from the solar array.

USER-CENTERED CONTROLS AND MONITORING

Refract House not only makes conservation and recycling of energy, water, and waste easy for the homeowner, but it also makes information about the users' habits readily accessible. A graphical monitoring DESIGNING FOR A station (Lucid Design Group's Building Dashboard) lets users SUSTAINABLE FUTURE track metrics for all three of these impacts, both in real time and historically. To accomplish this tracking, the house is extensively instrumented with flow and pressure sensors, environmental sensors, and devices to measure energy use and production. Energy and water usage rates are displayed on a customized, user-friendly website, which receives data every minute from sensors located throughout the house. A smartphone application allows users to remotely operate the lights and thermal control systems as well as monitor the performance of their house. These feedback loops help the homeowner actively understand, and then reduce, the house's environmental impact.

Everything about Refract House's materials—from the next-generation open-web bamboo I-joists to the selection of finishing materials—was considered from a lifecycle perspective. While this is seldom an easy or clear calculation, it was possible to make highly informed choices within the project limitations. Reflecting California's water scarcity, Refract House encourages minimal water consumption by having low-flow fixtures and equipment, hot-water recirculation, and a basin-style bathroom. A gray water reuse system allows for recycling water: "gray" water used in clothes washers, showers, and sinks is sent through a natural filtration process and reused for irrigation. These water-conscious measures have become an increasingly important part of green, sustainable building.

Refract House continues to teach us, our students, the public, and industry about what is on the horizon technologically in the realm of sustainable engineering design. Sustainability is about more than just energy independence. It is also about choosing materials carefully, minimizing water use, and encouraging the occupants of a building to be aware of their energy, water, and material consumption.

NOTES 1. The steel moment frames in Refract House are box-shaped frames comprised of two columns and two beams that have welded connections at the joints. These moment connections work together with the stiffness of the steel members to resist rotational forces and prevent the frame from racking.

2. The R value is a measure of thermal resistance used in the building and construction industry to determine the insulating value of materials and composite building wall, floor, and ceiling systems.

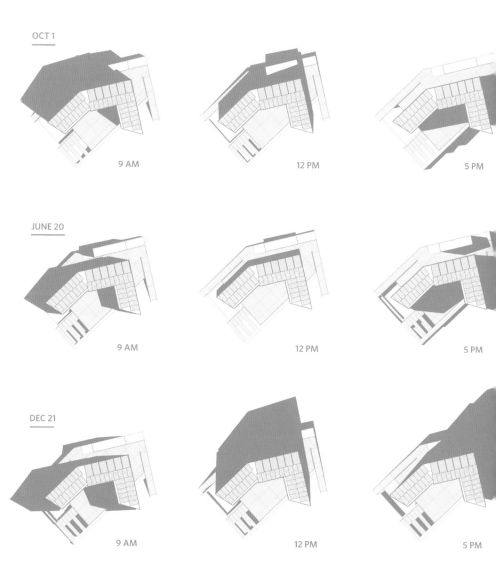

OCT 1

9 AM   12 PM   5 PM

JUNE 20

9 AM   12 PM   5 PM

DEC 21

9 AM   12 PM   5 PM

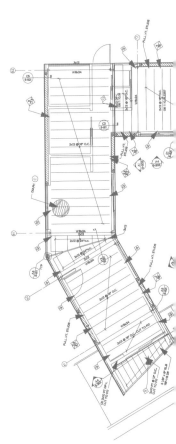

CARBON NEUTRAL DESIGN
KATE SIMONEN

Forward-thinking leaders in the building industry are increasingly looking to understand and reduce the environmental impact of built structures. The pressing challenge of climate change mitigation, coupled with the relative clarity of the carbon footprint as a concept, have made carbon increasingly interesting as a metric to designers, policy makers, and the public, and certainly to us as the makers of Refract House. However, as is often the case, something conceptually simple can be difficult to define and execute. What is carbon neutral design? Can a building actually be carbon neutral? What should our aspirations be in this realm?

"Carbon" is a simplified way of referring to the global warming potential of multiple greenhouse gases converted to an equivalent weight of CO_2 (CO_2e). Combustion energy (burning coal, gas, wood) is a major source of greenhouse gas emissions, and thus efforts to reduce these emissions often correlate with increasing energy efficiency in manufacturing pro-

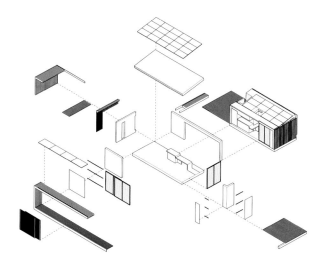

cesses and building operations. Processes such as the chemical reaction that forms concrete can release carbon; other processes, such as photosynthesis, can absorb it. Life Cycle Assessment (LCA) is a recognized method of tracking environmental impacts, such as carbon, over the full life cycle from "cradle" to "grave" (and ideally back to cradle again).[1] "Carbon neutral" describes a building or system in which the total carbon emitted over the entity's full life is equivalent to the carbon absorbed or eliminated (by offsetting or sequestering carbon).[2]

Given that nearly 50 percent of electrical energy use in the United States can be attributed to the building sector, a focus on operational impacts of buildings is appropriate and critical.[3] Projects such as Refract House help communicate currently available technologies to the general public and train the next generation of architects and engineers to be leaders in high-performance building design and renewable energy integration. As buildings become more energy efficient, the indirect environmental impacts from manufacturing and construction become more dominant. Given that the next 20 years are deemed to be critical for reducing CO_2, one can argue that focusing on the immediate impacts embodied in construction should have a high priority in industry practice.

Analysis of typical construction demonstrates that operational impacts such as heating, lighting, and equipment energy loads are usually the dominant contributor (in the range of 80 percent) to a building's total carbon footprint. It is technically feasible to design very-low-energy homes that incorporate sufficient on-site generation (such as solar panels) to offset energy usage. Refract House was designed to do this. Thus there are no greenhouse gas emissions attributed to the operation of the home, and

ABOVE
Exploded axonometric showing all building components of a single module of the Cap House prototype

OPPOSITE
Materials (left to right): compressed straw structural insulated panels [SIP]; stained/painted straw structural insulated panels; solar array; three-form eco-resin; reclaimed wood; SunPower solar panel

HEIGHT B

by some definitions this makes it "carbon neutral." This common definition is relatively straightforward to analyze and report, yet it omits impacts from other phases of the home's life such as manufacturing, construction, maintenance, and demolition.

Even if operational energy impacts are low, the impacts embodied in the materials of construction must be considered; indeed, when considered proportionally, relative to operational impacts, they can become very significant. Refract House is an extreme example of this. Given that its operational impacts are essentially net zero, ignoring the impacts associated with fabrication, transportation, erection, and demolition means ignoring more than 90 percent of the project's overall environmental impacts. Using LCA methodology, an inventory of materials, energy use, and activities (including trucking the house from California to Washington DC and back, plus round-trip plane flights for the team members) could be assembled, and the environmental impacts of each could be quantified and compiled to estimate the total impacts of construction. Depending on the method, database, and tools used, the calculation necessary to estimate the carbon footprint of the project would vary in complexity, accuracy, and effort. There are established and emerging methods to purchase a "carbon-offset," which aims to fund a project that reduces CO_2e to offset the carbon generated by a project so that the undertaking can be declared "carbon neutral."[4] However, even this expanded definition includes significant uncertainty in the computational assessments of both the carbon impact and the offset benefit.

The varying definitions of "carbon neutral" point to a key challenge in evaluating the environmental impact of the built environment: defining the scope of the assessment. Buildings can themselves be understood as systems, made up of many components. They can also, however, be understood as components of even larger systems: neighborhoods, cities, and regions. One could argue that a home could not be carbon neutral unless it was integrated into

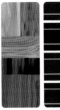

a carbon neutral region where issues of food production, transportation, play, and work were all integrated into a sustainable system with an overall neutral or even negative carbon footprint. As designers we must face the challenge of deeply engaging with the problem at hand (for instance, the design of a house) while simultaneously shaping the way our designs interface with and impact the broader ecosystem.

A conventional "attributional" LCA attributes impacts based on historical data to estimate the combined impacts of all processes used to create a product.[5] Designed originally to promote process improvement in manufacturing and assembly lines, this LCA methodology is today being translated to more complex products such as buildings and neighborhoods. A "consequential" LCA is an analysis that is forward looking and attempts to capture the consequences of a proposed change or action. In the LCA community, research in this area is most active with regard to biofuels. While an attributional LCA might demonstrate that biofuels have significantly reduced environmental impact based on comparisons between two fuel sources, a "consequential" LCA would require study and projection of the impact of changing crop types, or perhaps of cutting down forests to grow additional biofuel stock.

Assessing the environmental impacts of a Solar Decathlon house using solely attributional LCA methodology would be inappropriate because the goal of the Solar Decathlon is not just to build a house. The stated goals of the project are to educate student participants and the public about the many cost-saving opportunities presented by clean energy products, to demonstrate to the public the opportunities presented by the renewable energy systems that are available today, and to provide students with unique training to enter our nation's clean energy workforce.[6]

Assessing the environmental impacts of a Solar Decathlon house should include the consequences of its design and construction. Admittedly, these are difficult to quantify but interesting and important to consider. More than 70 students, 14 faculty members, and 12 professionals contributed to Refract House during the more than two-year process of design, analysis, construction, erection, use, dismantling, and review. Of these, how many will translate this gained knowledge, commitment, and expertise to impact other projects, clients, and colleagues? Of the more than 300,000 visitors to the National Mall, where the houses were on view, how many have been motivated to add insulation to their homes or install solar panels? Multiply this by the 20 teams that compete at each event, the multiple installations in the United States after the official event is over, and similar types of events executed and/or planned in Europe, Asia, and beyond, and the impacts certainly take on a different scale and complexity.

While we can aspire to design carbon neutral buildings, and work hard to understand and reduce carbon impacts throughout a building's life cycle, neutrality is not an objective but a strategy. As we work to reduce the environmental impact of the built environment, we hope to identify and target impacts most critical to sustaining life. But nonetheless, understanding the boundaries of our system, the scope of the problem, is essential to evaluating effects and assessing results. What is it we are trying to sustain? Most of us acknowledge that we cannot sustain ourselves indefinitely. How about our families, cities, society, and planet? Though we are now able to conceive of the complexities of interdependent systems, we still continue to simplify complexity in order to assess, communicate, and act.

Identifying and reducing the carbon impact of buildings is a critical and relevant effort. Defining certain buildings as carbon neutral risks oversimplifying complexity, obscuring critical relationships, and missing unintended consequences. Aspiring to create carbon neutral buildings, however, can lead us to engage in and take responsibility for further reduction of the environmental impact of the built environment. Here is where we should be placing our efforts: establishing performance targets, developing methods and tools to integrate LCA into the design process, and communicating the relevance and opportunities of low carbon design to our design professions, policy makers, and the public.

NOTES   1. For a conceptual framework, see William McDonough and Michael Braungart, *Cradle to Cradle: Remaking the Way We Make Things* (New York: North Point Press, 2002). For detailed technical requirements see the International Standards Organization LCA standards ISO 14025:2006, ISO 14040:2006, and ISO 14044:2006 (iso.org).

2. For more information see the Carbon Neutral Design Resource sponsored by the AIA and Society for Building Science Educators website, sbse.org/resources.

3. This estimate comes from the nonprofit organization Architecture 2030 (architecture2030.org), whose mission is the reduction of greenhouse gas emissions in the building sector.

4. For a good general description of current carbon offset methods, see the Rocky Mountain Institute Green Footstep tool (greenfootstep.org), which also includes links to additional resources on the topic.

5. For additional information on different LCA methods, see G. Finnveden, et al., "Recent Developments in Life Cycle Assessment," *Journal of Environmental Management* vol. 91 (2009): 1–21.

6. Per the U.S. Department of Energy Solar Decathlon website (solardecathlon.gov/about.html).

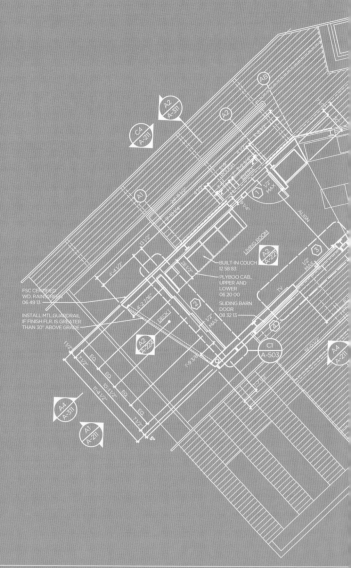

FSC CERTIFIED
WD. RAINSCREEN
06 49 13

INSTALL MTL.GUARDRAIL
IF FINISH FLR. IS GREATER
THAN 30" ABOVE GRADE

BUILT-IN COUCH
12 58 83

PLYBOO CAB.
UPPER AND
LOWER
06 20 00

SLIDING BARN
DOOR
08 32 13

A1 | FLOOR PLAN MODULE A

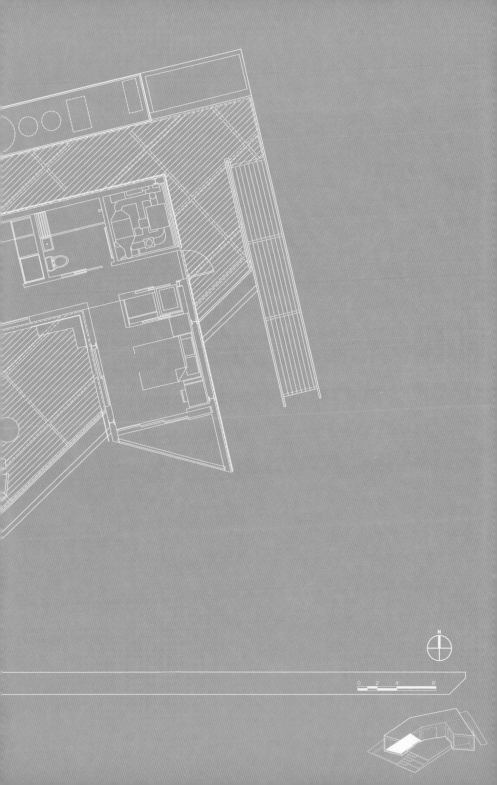

N

0 2' 4' 8'

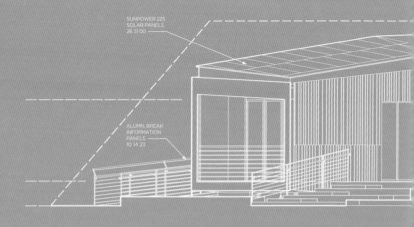

SUNPOWER 225
SOLAR PANELS
26 31 00

ALUMN. BREAK
INFORMATION
PANELS
10 14 23

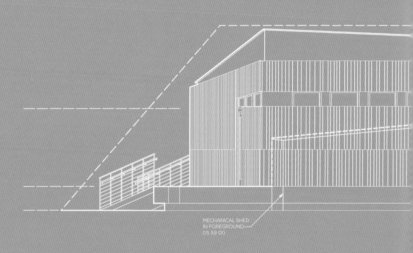

MECHANICAL SHED
IN FOREGROUND
05 59 00

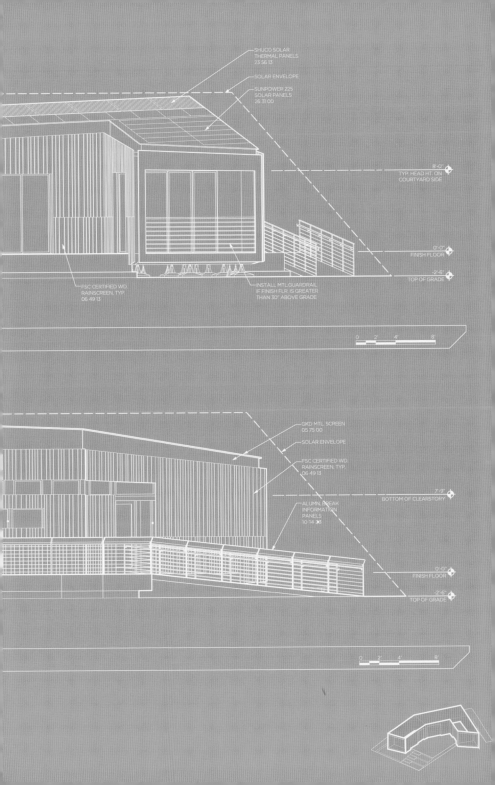

SHUCO SOLAR
THERMAL PANELS
23 56 13

SOLAR ENVELOPE

SUNPOWER 225
SOLAR PANELS
26 31 00

8'-0"
TYP. HEAD HT. ON
COURTYARD SIDE

0'-0"
FINISH FLOOR

-2'-6"
TOP OF GRADE

FSC CERTIFIED WD.
RAINSCREEN, TYP.
06 49 13

INSTALL MTL GUARDRAIL
IF FINISH FLR. IS GREATER
THAN 30" ABOVE GRADE

0   2   4   8'

GKD MTL. SCREEN
05 75 00

SOLAR ENVELOPE

FSC CERTIFIED WD.
RAINSCREEN, TYP.
06 49 13

7'-9"
BOTTOM OF CLEARSTORY

ALUMN. BREAK
INFORMATION
PANELS
10 14 13

0'-0"
FINISH FLOOR

-2'-6"
TOP OF GRADE

0   2'   4'   8'

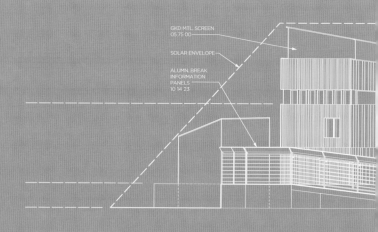

GKD MTL. SCREEN
05 75 00

SOLAR ENVELOPE

ALUMN. BREAK
INFORMATION
PANELS
10 14 23

| C1 | ENTRY ELEVATION |

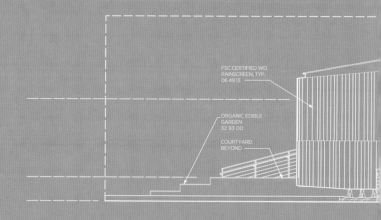

FSC CERTIFIED WD.
RAINSCREEN, TYP.
06 49 13

ORGANIC EDIBLE
GARDEN
32 93 00

COURTYARD
BEYOND

| A1 | EAST ELEVATION |

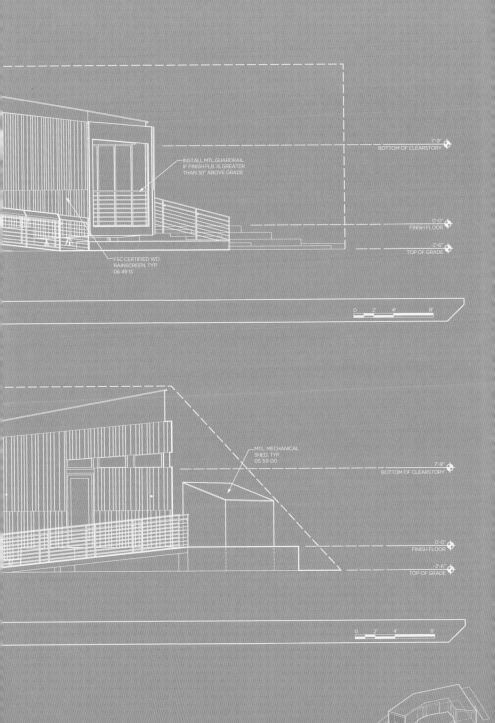

INSTALL MTL. GUARDRAIL
IF FINISH FLR. IS GREATER
THAN 30" ABOVE GRADE

7'-9"
BOTTOM OF CLEARSTORY

0'-0"
FINISH FLOOR

-2'-6"
TOP OF GRADE

FSC CERTIFIED WD.
RAINSCREEN, TYP.
06 49 13

0   2'   4'   8'

MTL. MECHANICAL
SHED, TYP.
05 59 00

7'-9"
BOTTOM OF CLEARSTORY

0'-0"
FINISH FLOOR

-2'-6"
TOP OF GRADE

0   2'   4'   8'

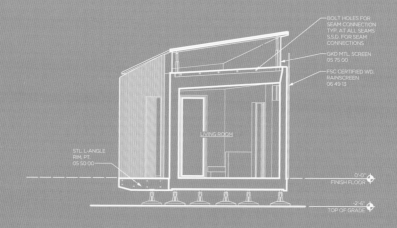

BOLT HOLES FOR
SEAM CONNECTION
TYP. AT ALL SEAMS
S.S.D. FOR SEAM
CONNECTIONS

GKD MTL. SCREEN
05 75 00

FSC CERTIFIED WD.
RAINSCREEN
06 49 13

LIVING ROOM

STL. L-ANGLE
RIM, PT.
05 50 00

0'-0"
FINISH FLOOR

-2'-6"
TOP OF GRADE

C1   SEAM MODULE A

0   2'   4'   8'

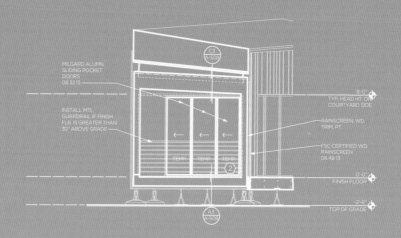

MILGARD ALUMN.
SLIDING POCKET
DOORS
08 32 13

INSTALL MTL.
GUARDRAIL IF FINISH
FLR. IS GREATER THAN
30" ABOVE GRADE

C3
A-508

8'-0"
TYP. HEAD HT. ON
COURTYARD SIDE

RAINSCREEN, WD.
TRIM, PT.

FSC CERTIFIED WD.
RAINSCREEN
06 49 13

TEMP.   TEMP.   TEMP.

0'-0"
FINISH FLOOR

-2'-6"
TOP OF GRADE

A2   ENDCAP MODULE A

0   2'   4'   8'

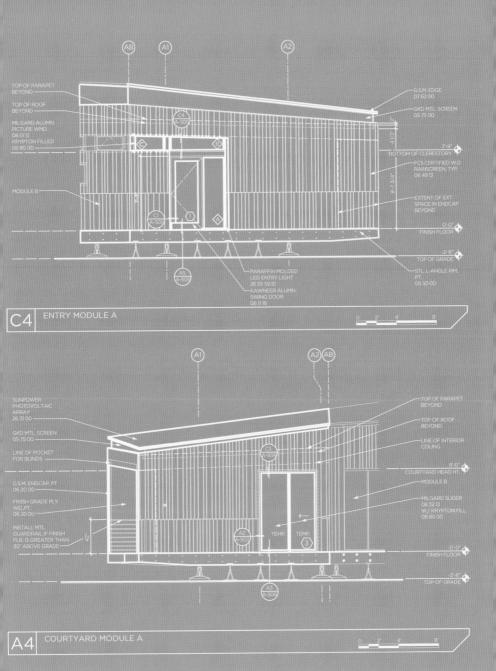

AB   A1   A2

TOP OF PARAPET
BEYOND

TOP OF ROOF
BEYOND

MILGARD ALUMN.
PICTURE WND.
08 51 13
KRYPTON FILLED
08 80 00

MODULE B

G.S.M. EDGE
07 62 00

GKD MTL. SCREEN
05 75 00

7'-9"
BOTTOM OF CLERESTORY

FCS CERTIFIED W.D
RAINSCREEN, TYP.
06 49 13

EXTENT OF EXT.
SPACE IN ENDCAP
BEYOND

0'-0"
FINISH FLOOR

-2'-6"
TOP OF GRADE

STL L-ANGLE RIM,
PT.
05 50 00

PARAFFIN MOLDED
LED ENTRY LIGHT
26 55 59.10

KAWNEER ALUMN.
SWING DOOR
08 11 16

C4 ENTRY MODULE A

0   2   4   8

A1   A2 AB

SUNPOWER
PHOTOVOLTAIC
ARRAY
26 31 00

GKD MTL. SCREEN
05 75 00

LINE OF POCKET
FOR BLINDS

G.S.M. ENDCAP, PT
06 20 00

FINISH GRADE PLY
WD, PT.
06 20 00

INSTALL MTL.
GUARDRAIL IF FINISH
FLR. IS GREATER THAN
30" ABOVE GRADE

42"

TOP OF PARAPET
BEYOND

TOP OF ROOF
BEYOND

LINE OF INTERIOR
CEILING

8'-0"
COURTYARD HEAD HT.

MODULE B

MILGARD SLIDER
08 32 13
W./ KRYPTON FILL
08 80 00

TEMP.   TEMP.
3

0'-0"
FINISH FLOOR

-2'-6"
TOP OF GRADE

A4 COURTYARD MODULE A

0   2   4   8

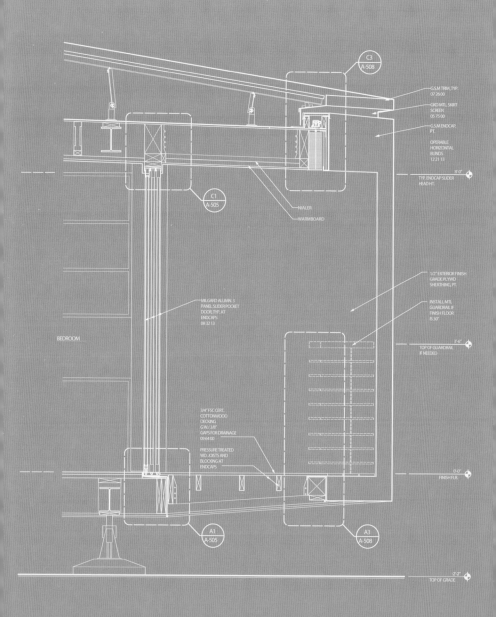

G.S.M TRIM ,TYP.
07 26 00

GRD.MTL. SKIRT
SCREEN
05 75 00

G.S.M ENDCAP.
PT.

OPERABLE
HORIZONTAL
BLINDS
12 21 13

8'-0"
TYP. ENDCAP SLIDER
HEAD HT.

C3
A-508

NAILER

WARMBOARD

C1
A-505

1/2" EXTERIOR FINISH
GRADE PLYWD
SHEATHING, PT.

INSTALL MTL
GUARDRAIL IF
FINISH FLOOR
IS 30"

3'-6"
TOP OF GUARDRAIL
IF NEEDED

MILGARD ALUMN. 3
PANEL SLIDER POCKET
DOOR, TYP. AT
ENDCAPS
08 32 13

BEDROOM

3/4" FSC CERT.
COTTONWOOD
DECKING
G.W. 3/8"
GAPS FOR DRAINAGE
09 64 00

PRESSURE TREATED
WD. JOISTS AND
BLOCKING AT
ENDCAPS

0'-0"
FINISH FLR.

A1
A-505

A3
A-508

-3'-2"
TOP OF GRADE

A1   TYPICAL LONGITUDINAL AT ENDCAPS

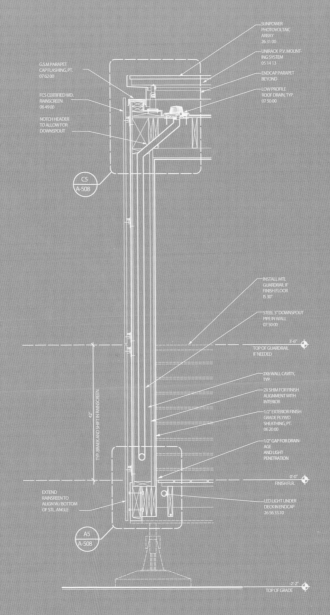

SUNPOWER
PHOTOVOLTAIC
ARRAY
26 31 00

UNIRACK P.V. MOUNT-
ING SYSTEM
05 14 13

ENDCAP PARAPET
BEYOND

G.S.M PARAPET
CAP FLASHING, PT.
07 62 00

LOW PROFILE
ROOF DRAIN, TYP.
07 50 00

FCS CERTIFIED WD.
RAINSCREEN
06 49 00

NOTCH HEADER
TO ALLOW FOR
DOWNSPOUT

C5
A-508

INSTALL MTL.
GUARDRAIL IF
FINISH FLOOR
IS 30"

STEEL 3" DOWNSPOUT
PIPE IN WALL
07 50 00

3'-6"
TOP OF GUARDRAIL
IF NEEDED

2X6 WALL CAVITY,
TYP.

2X SHIM FOR FINISH
ALIGNMENT WITH
INTERIOR

1/2" EXTERIOR FINISH
GRADE PLYWD
SHEATHING, PT.
06 20 00

1/2" GAP FOR DRAIN-
AGE
AND LIGHT
PENETRATION

TYP. 8°KICK AND SHIFT IN RAINSCREEN

42"

0'-0"
FINISH FLR.

EXTEND
RAINSCREEN TO
ALIGN W/ BOTTOM
OF STL. ANGLE

LED LIGHT UNDER
DECK IN ENDCAP
26 56 33.10

A5
A-508

-2'-2"
TOP OF GRADE

A5 | TYPICAL ENDCAP W/ ROOF DRAIN

0   1/2"   1'   2'

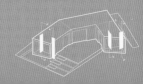

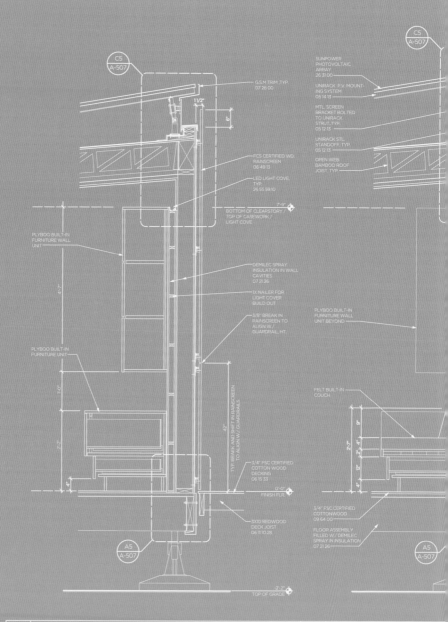

CS
A-507

CS
A-507

G.S.M. TRIM, TYP.
07 26 00

SUNPOWER
PHOTOVOLTAIC
ARRAY
26 31 00

UNIRACK P.V. MOUNT-
ING SYSTEM
05 14 13

MTL. SCREEN
BRACKET BOLTED
TO UNIRACK
STRUT, TYP.
05 12 13

FCS CERTIFIED WD.
RAINSCREEN
06 49 13

UNIRACK STL.
STANDOFF, TYP.
05 12 13

OPEN WEB
BAMBOO ROOF
JOIST, TYP.

LED LIGHT COVE,
TYP.
26 55 59.10

BOTTOM OF CLEARSTORY /
TOP OF CASEWORK /
LIGHT COVE

PLYBOO BUILT-IN
FURNITURE WALL
UNIT

DEMILEC SPRAY
INSULATION IN WALL
CAVITIES
07 21 26

1X NAILER FOR
LIGHT COVER
BUILD OUT

PLYBOO BUILT-IN
FURNITURE WALL
UNIT BEYOND

3/8" BREAK IN
RAINSCREEN TO
ALIGN W /
GUARDRAIL, HT.

PLYBOO BUILT-IN
FURNITURE UNIT

FELT BUILT-IN
COUCH

TYP. BREAK AND SHIFT IN RAINSCREEN
TO ALIGN W/ GUARDRAILS

1/4" FSC CERTIFIED
COTTON WOOD
DECKING
06 15 33

0'-0"
FINISH FLR.

1/4" FSC CERTIFIED
COTTONWOOD
09 64 00

FLOOR ASSEMBLY
FILLED W / DEMILEC
SPRAY IN INSULATION
07 21 26

A5
A-507

3X10 REDWOOD
DECK JOIST
06 11 10.26

A5
A-507

-2'-2"
TOP OF GRADE

A1 NON-COURTYARD THRU. TYP. WALL/CAB.

A3 NON-COURTYARD THRU. COUC

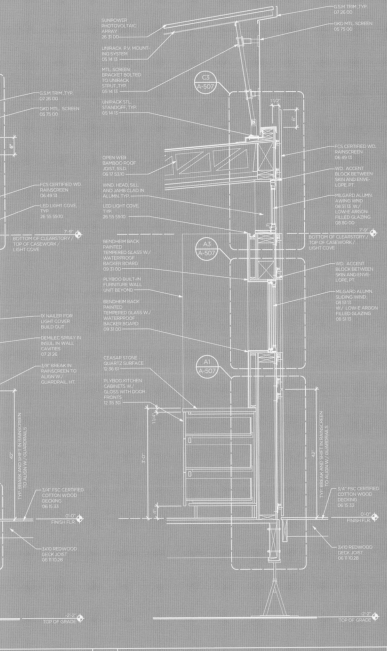

SUNPOWER
PHOTOVOLTAIC
ARRAY
26 31 00

UNIRACK P.V. MOUNT-
ING SYSTEM
05 14 13

MTL. SCREEN
BRACKET BOLTED
TO UNIRACK
STRUT, TYP.
05 14 13

G.S.M TRIM, TYP.
07 26 00

SKD MTL. SCREEN
05 75 00

UNIRACK STL.
STANDOFF, TYP.
05 14 13

C3
A-507

G.S.M TRIM, TYP.
07 26 00

SKD MTL. SCREEN
05 75 00

1 1/2"

6"

FCS CERTIFIED WD.
RAINSCREEN
06 49 13

WD. ACCENT
BLOCK BETWEEN
SKIN AND ENVE-
LOPE, PT.

MILGARD ALUM.
AWNING WND.
08 51 13 W/
LOW-E ARGON
FILLED GLAZING
08 80 00

6"

OPEN WEB
BAMBOO ROOF
JOIST, S.S.D.
06 17 53.10

FCS CERTIFIED WD.
RAINSCREEN
06 49 13

WND. HEAD, SILL
AND JAMB CLAD IN
ALUMN. TYP.

LED LIGHT COVE,
TYP.
26 55 59.10

LED LIGHT COVE,
TYP.
26 55 59.10

7'-9"

BOTTOM OF CLEARSTORY /
TOP OF CASEWORK /
LIGHT COVE

A3
A-507

7'-9"

BOTTOM OF CLEARSTORY /
TOP OF CASEWORK /
LIGHT COVE

BENDHEIM BACK
PAINTED
TEMPERED GLASS W/
WATERPROOF
BACKER BOARD
09 31 00

WD. ACCENT
BLOCK BETWEEN
SKIN AND ENVE-
LOPE, PT.

1X NAILER FOR
LIGHT COVER
BUILD OUT

PLYBOO BUILT-IN
FURNITURE WALL
UNIT BEYOND

MILGARD ALUM.
SLIDING WIND.
08 51 13
W/ LOW-E ARGON
FILLED GLAZING
08 51 13

DEMILEC SPRAY IN
INSUL. IN WALL
CAVITIES
07 21 26

BENDHEIM BACK
PAINTED
TEMPERED GLASS W/
WATERPROOF
BACKER BOARD
09 31 00

3/8" BREAK IN
RAINSCREEN TO
ALIGN W/
GUARDRAIL. HT.

A1
A-507

CEASAR STONE
QUARTZ SURFACE
12 36 61

PLYBOO KITCHEN
CABINETS W/
GLOSS WITH DOOR
FRONTS
12 35 30

1 1/4"

3'-0"

42"

TYP. BREAK AND SHIFT IN RAINSCREEN
TO ALIGN W/ GUARDRAILS

42"

TYP. BREAK AND SHIFT IN RAINSCREEN
TO ALIGN W/ GUARDRAILS

3/4" FSC CERTIFIED
COTTON WOOD
DECKING
06 15 33

3/4" FSC CERTIFIED
COTTON WOOD
DECKING
06 15 33

0'-0"
FINISH FLR.

0'-0"
FINISH FLR.

3X10 REDWOOD
DECK JOIST
06 11 10.28

3X10 REDWOOD
DECK JOIST
06 11 10.28

-2'-2"
TOP OF GRADE

-2'-2"
TOP OF GRADE

A5   NON-COURTYARD THRU. KITCHEN WNDS.

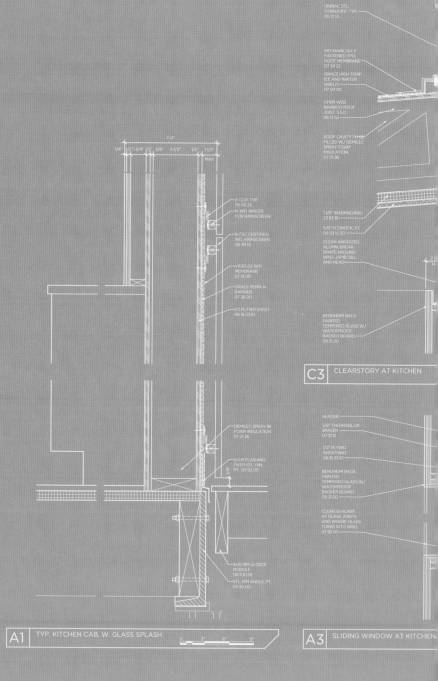

UNIRAC STL.
STANDOFF, TYP.
05 12 13

MECHANICALLY
FASTENED TPO.
ROOF MEMBRANE
07 54 23

GRACE HIGH TEMP.
ICE AND WATER
SHIELD
07 50 00

OPEN WEB
BAMBOO ROOF
JOIST, S.S.D.
06 17 53

ROOF CAVITY TO BE
FILLED W/ DEMILEC
SPRAY FOAM
INSULATION.
07 21 26

1 1/8" WARMBOARD
23 83 16

5/8" ECOROCK, PT.
09 29 10.30

CLEAR ANODIZED
ALUMN. BREAK
SHAPE AROUND
WND. JAMB, SILL
AND HEAD

BENDHEIM BACK
PAINTED
TEMPERED GLASS W/
WATERPROOF
BACKER BOARD
09 31 00

C3 CLEARSTORY AT KITCHEN

Z-CLIP, TYP.
05 05 23

1x WD. NAILER
FOR RAINSCREEN

1x FSC CERTIFIED
WD. RAINSCREEN
06 49 13

VIDIFLEX W.P.
MEMBRANE
07 13 00

GRACE PERM-A-
BARRIER
07 26 00

1/2 PLYWD SHEET
06 16 23.10

HEADER

3/8" THERMABLOK
SPACER
07 21 13

1/2" PLYWD
SHEATHING
06 16 23.10

BENDHEIM BACK
PAINTED
TEMPERED GLASS W/
WATERPROOF
BACKER BOARD
09 31 00

CLEAR SEALANT
AT GLASS JOINTS
AND WHERE GLASS
TURNS INTO WND.
07 92 00

DEMILEC SPRAY IN
FOAM INSULATION
07 21 26

G.S.M. FLASHING
OVER STL. RIM,
PT. 07 62 00

3x10 RIM @ DECK
MODULE
06 11 10.28

STL. RIM ANGLE, PT.
05 50 00

A1 TYP. KITCHEN CAB. W. GLASS SPLASH

A3 SLIDING WINDOW AT KITCHEN

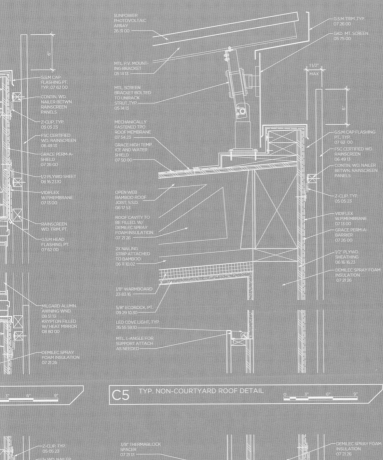

SUNPOWER
PHOTOVOLTAIC
ARRAY
26 31 00

G.S.M. TRIM, TYP.
07 26 00

GRD. MT. SCREEN
05 75 00

MTL. P.V. MOUNT-
ING BRACKET
05 14 13

MTL. SCREEN
BRACKET BOLTED
TO UNIRACK
STRUT, TYP.
05 14 12

1 1/2"
MAX

G.S.M. CAP FLASHING
PT., TYP.
07 62 00

MECHANICALLY
FASTENED TPO
ROOF MEMBRANE
07 54 23

FSC CERTIFIED WD.
RAINSCREEN
06 49 13

GRACE HIGH TEMP.
ICE AND WATER
SHIELD
07 50 00

CONTIN. WD. NAILER
BETWN. RAINSCREEN
PANELS

OPEN WEB
BAMBOO ROOF
JOIST, S.S.D.
06 17 53

Z-CLIP, TYP.
05 05 23

ROOF CAVITY TO
BE FILLED W/
DEMILEC SPRAY
FOAM INSULATION
07 21 26

VIDIFLEX
W.P.MEMBRANE
07 13 00

2X NAILING
STRIP ATTACHED
TO BAMBOO
06 11 10.02

GRACE PERM-A-
BARRIER
07 26 00

1/8" WARMBOARD
23 83 16

1/2" PLYWD.
SHEATHING
06 16 23

5/8" ECOROCK, PT.
09 29 10.30

DEMILEC SPRAY FOAM
INSULATION
07 21 26

LED COVE LIGHT, TYP.
26 55 59.10

MTL. L-ANGLE FOR
SUPPORT ATTACH
AS NEEDED

G.S.M. CAP
FLASHING, PT.,
TYP. 07 62 00

CONTIN. WD.
NAILER BETWN.
RAINSCREEN
PANELS

Z-CLIP, TYP.
05 05 23

FSC CERTIFIED
WD. RAINSCREEN
06 49 13

GRACE PERM-A-
SHIELD
07 26 00

1/2" PLYWD SHEET
06 16 23.10

VIDIFLEX
W.P.MEMBRANE
07 13 00

RAINSCREEN
WD. TRIM, PT.

G.S.M. HEAD
FLASHING, PT.
07 62 00

MILGARD ALUMN.
AWNING WND.
08 51 13
KRYPTON FILLED
W/ HEAT MIRROR
08 80 00

DEMILEC SPRAY
FOAM INSULATION
07 21 26

| C5 | TYP. NON-COURTYARD ROOF DETAIL |

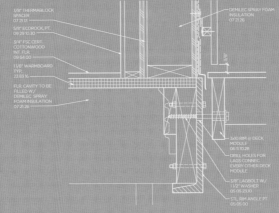

Z-CLIP, TYP.
05 05 23

1x WD. NAILER
FOR RAINSCREEN

1x FSC CERTIFIED
WD. RAINSCREEN
06 49 13

RAINSCREEN
WD. TRIM, PT.

1/8" THERMABLOCK
SPACER
07 21 15

5/8" ECOROCK, PT.
09 29 10.30

3/4" FSC CERT.
COTTONWOOD
INT. FLR.
09 64 00

1 1/8" WARMBOARD
TYP.
23 83 16

FLR. CAVITY TO BE
FILLED W/
DEMILEC SPRAY
FOAM INSULATION
07 21 26

DEMILEC SPRAY FOAM
INSULATION
07 21 26

5x10 RIM @ DECK
MODULE
06 11 10.28

DRILL HOLES FOR
LAGS CONNECT
EVERY OTHER DECK
MODULE

3/8" LAGBOLT W./
1 1/2" WASHER
05 05 23.10

STL. RIM ANGLE PT
05 05 00

DEMILEC SPRAY FOAM
INSULATION 07 21 26

| A5 | TYP. NON-COURTYARD SILL DETAIL |

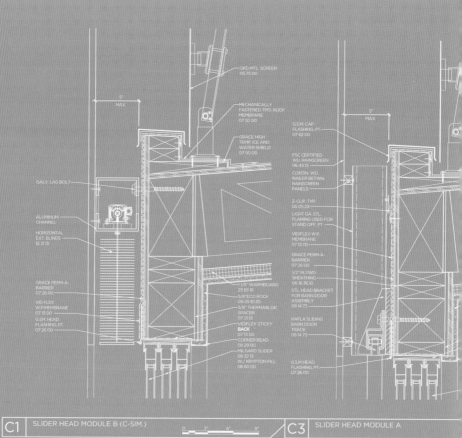

GKD MTL. SCREEN
05 75 00

MECHANICALLY
FASTENED TPO. ROOF
MEMBRANE
07 50 00

GRACE HIGH
TEMP. ICE AND
WATER SHIELD
07 50 00

GALV. LAG BOLT

ALUMINIUM
CHANNEL

HORIZONTAL
EXT. BLINDS
12 21 13

GRACE PERM-A-
BARRIER
07 26 00

VID FLEX
W.P. MEMBRANE
07 13 00

G.S.M. HEAD
FLASHING, PT.
07 26 00

1 7/8" WARMBOARD
23 83 16
5/8" ECO ROCK
09 29 10.30
3/8" THERMABLOK
SPACER
07 21 13
VIDIFLEX STICKY
BACK
07 13 00
CORNER BEAD
09 29 00
MILGARD SLIDER
08 32 13
W/ KRYPTON FILL
08 80 00

G.S.M. CAP
FLASHING, PT.
07 62 00

FSC CERTIFIED
WD. RAINSCREEN
06 49 13

CONTIN. WD.
NAILER BETWN.
RAINSCREEN
PANELS

Z-CLIP, TYP.
05 05 23

LIGHT GA. STL.
FLASHING USED FOR
STAND OFF, PT.

VIDIFLEX W.P.
MEMBRANE
07 13 00

GRACE PERM-A-
BARRIER
07 26 00

1/2" PLYWD
SHEATHING
06 16 36.10

STL. HEAD BRACKET
FOR BARN DOOR
ASSEMBLY
08 14 73

HAFLA SLIDING
BARN DOOR
TRACK
08 14 73

G.S.M. HEAD
FLASHING, PT.
07 26 00

C1 SLIDER HEAD MODULE B (C-SIM.)   0 3" 6" 9"   **C3** SLIDER HEAD MODULE A

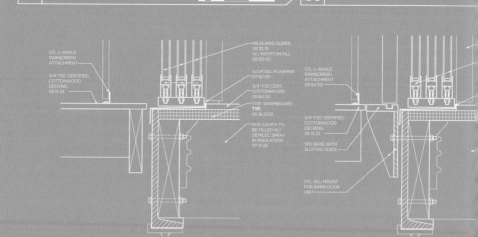

STL. L-ANGLE
RAINSCREEN
ATTACHMENT

3/4" FSC CERTIFIED
COTTONWOOD
DECKING
06 15 33

MILGUARD SLIDER
08 32 13
W/ KRYPTON FILL
08 80 00

G.S.M. SILL FLASHING
07 62 00

3/4" FSC CERT.
COTTONWOOD
09 64 00

1 1/8" WARMBOARD
TYP.
06 16 23.10

PUR. CAVITY TO
BE FILLED W/
DEMILEC SPRAY
IN INSULATION
07 21 26

STL. L-ANGLE
RAINSCREEN
ATTACHMENT
09 64 00

3/4" FSC CERTIFIED
COTTONWOOD
DECKING
06 15 33

WD. BASE WITH
SLOTTED GUIDE

STL. SILL MOUNT
FOR BARN DOOR
UNIT

A1 SLIDER SILL MODULE B (C-SIM.)   0 3" 6"   **A3** SLIDER SILL MODULE A

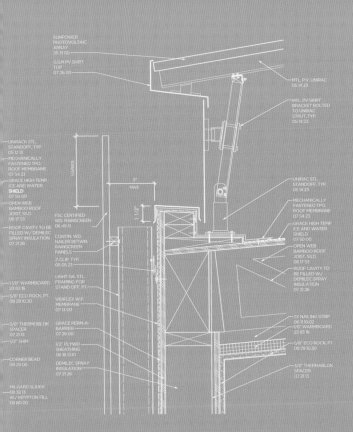

SUNPOWER
PHOTOVOLTAIC
ARRAY
26 31 00

G.S.M PV SKIRT
TOP
07 26 00

MTL. P.V. UNIRAC
05 14 23

MTL. PV SKIRT
BRACKET BOLTED
TO UNIRAC
STRUT, TYP.
05 14 23

UNIRACK STL.
STANDOFF, TYP.
05 12 13

MECHANICALLY
FASTENED TPO.
ROOF MEMBRANE
07 54 23

GRACE HIGH TEMP.
ICE AND WATER
SHIELD
07 50 00

OPEN WEB
BAMBOO ROOF
JOIST, SS.D.
06 17 53

ROOF CAVITY TO BE
FILLED W./ DEMILEC
SPRAY INSULATION
07 21 26

FSC CERTIFIED
WD. RAINSCREEN
06 49 13

CONTIN. WD.
NAILER BETWN.
RAINSCREEN
PANELS

Z-CLIP, TYP.
05 05 23

LIGHT GA. STL.
FRAMING FOR
STAND OFF, PT.

VIDIFLEX W.P.
MEMBRANE
07 13 00

GRACE PERM-A-
BARRIER
07 26 00

1/2" PLYWD
SHEATHING
06 16 13 10

DEMILEC SPRAY
INSULATION
07 21 26

UNIRAC STL
STANDOFF, TYP.
05 14 23

MECHANICALLY
FASTENED TPO.
ROOF MEMBRANE
07 54 23

GRACE HIGH TEMP.
ICE AND WATER
SHIELD
07 50 00

OPEN WEB
BAMBOO ROOF
JOIST, SS.D.
06 17 53

ROOF CAVITY TO
BE FILLED W./
DEMILEC SPRAY
INSULATION
07 21 26

2X NAILING STRIP
06 11 10 02

1/8" WARMBOARD
23 83 16

5/8" ECO ROCK, PT.
09 29 10 30

3/8" THERMOBLOK
SPACER
07 21 13

1 1/8" WARMBOARD
23 83 16

5/8" ECO ROCK, PT.
09 29 10 30

3/8" THERMOBLOK
SPACER
07 21 13

1/2" SHIM

CORNER BEAD
09 29 00

MILGARD SLIDER
08 32 13
W./ KRYPTON FILL
08 80 00

VARIES

5"
MAX

1 1/2"

___9"___ | **C5** | TYP. COURTYARD ROOF CONNECTION   0   3"   6"   9"

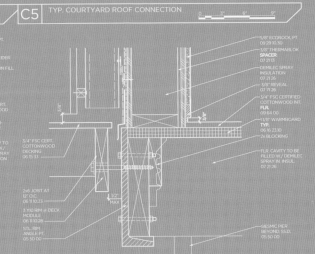

ECOROCK, PT.
BEYOND
09 29 00

MILGARD SLIDER
08 32 13
W./ KRYPTON FILL
08 80 00

G.S.M SILL
FLASHING
07 62 00

3/4" FSC CERT.
COTTONWOOD
09 64 00

1 1/8" WARM-
BOARD TYP.
06 16 23 10

FLR. CAVITY TO BE
FILLED W./
DEMILEC SPRAY
IN INSULATION
07 21 26

3/4" FSC CERT.
COTTONWOOD
DECKING
06 15 33

2x6 JOIST AT
12" O.C.
06 11 10 23

3 X10 RIM @ DECK
MODULE
06 11 10 28

STL. RIM
ANGLE PT.
05 50 00

5/8" ECOROCK, PT
09 29 10 30

3/8" THERMABLOK
SPACER
07 21 13

DEMILEC SPRAY
INSULATION
07 21 26

3/8" REVEAL
07 21 26

3/4" FSC CERTIFIED
COTTONWOOD INT.
FLR.
09 64 00

1 1/8" WARMBOARD
TYP.
06 16 23 30

2x BLOCKING

FLR. CAVITY TO BE
FILLED W./ DEMILEC
SPRAY IN INSUL.
07 21 26

SEISMIC PIER
BEYOND, SS.D.
05 50 00

3/8"

5/8"

1/2"
MAX

___9"___ | **A5** | TYP. COURTYARD SILL CONNECTION   0   3"   6"   9"

MATERIAL
FABRICATION

CONSTRUCTION INNOVATION
PETER ANDERSON

The application of emerging technology to the process of designing and building is bringing many changes to the way we work and the way we think about the roles of everyone involved in making things. Some changes are incremental, such as steady improvements in building insulation and enclosure systems, and some are more transformative, such as digital tools for the modeling of complex forms or the modeling of building performance. But the most exciting opportunities wrought by technological change lie in the process of project realization, and the ways in which approaches to fabrication, and more specifically prefabrication, can be extended to embrace far broader applications.

The simplest forms of prefabrication have always been essential to architecture. The selection of raw materials, and then the subsequent selection of techniques for their modification into building components, PREFABRICATION inevitably derive from the proximity of resources to the intended location of the finished building. Even when distances are short and fabrication is

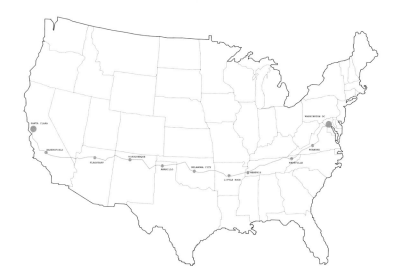

not complex, there are stages of prefabrication that allow for working on materials in one place, then transporting them to another place for final assembly with other components. In the felling of trees for making log structures, for example, it is most efficient to remove the bark and branches where the trees fall, and perhaps also to cut the logs into rough module lengths, before moving them to the building site. More detailed hewing of mating surfaces and corner connections might happen nearer or adjacent to the site, prior to actual assembly. Similarly, ancient civilizations would quarry stone from the closest suitable source, cutting or breaking it into sizes and configurations amenable to transport and building use. These concepts of prefabrication are no different from our current situation; it is just that the number of stages, levels of refinement, and degree of aggregate assembly at each stage have increased.

Since the beginning of the industrial age, the efficiency of and multiple options for transport have widened the range of possible sources of raw and component materials for a particular project, and the extent of fabrication of those materials has become greater. This allows for multiple stages of processing, locationally determined by the availability of materials and appropriate labor or machinery, leading to ever-greater areas of specialization and links in the process, which in turn allows for the creation of increasingly complex subassemblies manufactured at physically distinct locations, which must then be transported, combined with other pieces, and then moved again, through multiple iterations in the process of transformation, assembly, and transport, before arriving at and becoming part of a fixed building structure.

This understanding of prefabrication is an incremental expansion of logical construction processes in continual development since humans first began to use tools. Today we have a global network of BUILDING SUBASSEMBLIES resources, fabricators, and collaborators, available for thoughtful integration into architectural works. Of course just because we can prefabricate doesn't necessarily mean that we always should prefabricate, and our ever-increasing access to global resources requires that we make wise decisions about when, where, and how to tap into those resources, weighing a wide array of inputs such as financial and environmental costs as well as issues of developmental economics, social justice, cultural continuity, and geopolitical stability. Prefabrication of building components happens in many different ways, and there is an important role for architects in the direction and selection of construction methods, studied from a position of broad consciousness of the diverse implications.

One of the primary hallmarks of industrialization is the inherent efficiency of multiple production of the same, or similar, pieces, which was so importantly exploited by Henry Ford in production lines for the Model T. The factory-line trajectory pushed forward by Ford led to continual improvement over the last century in the quality and affordability of automobiles, if not, at least in the early stages, in the encouragement of creative diversity. The same trajectory of progress in process can be seen in all areas of material production, from consumer goods such as shoes to airplanes and computers. Inherent in the nature of multiple production is the opportunity for iterative improvement—in design and in process—since the investment in

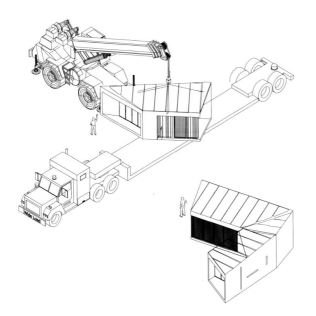

research and improvement is cost-effectively distributed over the resulting quantity of production. While this progressive notion of continual improvement in quality and efficiency can be seen to bear fruit in almost all areas of human endeavor, there are some industry sectors that embrace and utilize it more effectively than others. It is certainly worthwhile to make a critical evaluation of how we utilize this opportunity for continual improvement and research in the practice and realization of architecture, with the hope of learning to better channel our efforts into the making of our current projects, and of capturing iterative improvement expectations in architecture and construction.

It is frequently said that the construction industry has never been able to succeed in the mass production of buildings. The grandly failed factory-produced-home schemes of Walter Gropius and **INDUSTRIALIZED COMPONENTS** Konrad Wachsmann, or the Lustron or Dymaxion homes, are cited as cautionary tales about how and why mass production is not feasible for the buildings in which we live and work. This historical observation may be missing the point, however, as it ignores related areas of tremendous progress in the industrialized manufacture of building components, and the extent to which our buildings are now modularized and standardized. Windows, doors, plywood, flooring, metal siding, furniture, appliances, and lighting fixtures are all mass-produced in highly automated and efficient factories throughout the world. Mass production,

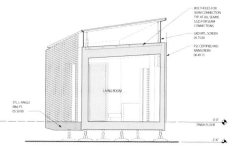

and the increasing flexibility of industrial production recognized in the potential for mass customization, provides architects with an enormous palette of products to choose from in designing buildings—a fully industrialized kit of parts that can be used to make almost any kind of building, with ever-decreasing necessity for design of hand-crafted and one-off custom componentry. In many ways, architects are missing opportunities for more productive engagement with industry, generally accepting a common perception of an incompatibility between modularized, multiple production and the potentials for creative architecture.

ABOVE
Section through seam connection between living room (module A) and kitchen (module B)

OPPOSITE
The truck putting down the house

One of the most interesting aspects of the Solar Decathlon competition is that the rules require the entries to be capable of, and planned for, multiple production, even while the buildings presented for exhibition would mostly fall into the category of custom, one-off designs or first-stage prototypes,

with the teams devoting relatively little attention to gathering the process information that would allow improvement in further built iterations. Regardless of whether the designs are in fact built again, the presupposition that they should be able to be, and might be, is an important design parameter and conceptual framework that could well be employed more broadly in the field of architecture in general. This would encourage greater utilization of iterative design feedback processes as a way to integrate continual improvement concepts into our architectural production, and expand the beneficial role and impact of the architect, both within and beyond our profession, in decisions at every stage of the design, production, and performance analysis of building components and assemblies. The software and hardware tools now routinely available to architects make it ever more possible to design, prototype, fabricate, then redesign, reprototype, and refabricate, and thus to iteratively improve parts and pieces of architecture. This could initiate a much broader understanding of the architect's role in making and critically developing the built environment, thereby beneficially intermingling the processes of design, prototyping, and production into a broader definition of the concept of prefabrication.

The potential for iterative development inherent in processes of construction systemization and prefabrication can only be fully harnessed in a collaborative relationship maintaining through all phases of the project, from design to construction to critical performance review and then to well-informed design improvements for the next unit. This process of improvement is not well engaged in the common architecture, engineering, and construction industry relationships, in which the interests of all these parties are intentionally divided. Often referred to as a design-bid-build approach, this typical industry practice sets the architect and builder into a relatively adversarial relationship, so that information proceeds in a linear fashion, critical performance review is disadvantageous and avoided, and learning is neither well-integrated into the current project nor easily carried forward into future projects.

The cooperative relationship between architect and builder known as design-build, and the newer conception of this cooperative project relationship referred to as Integrated Project Delivery, or IPD, are **DESIGN-BUILD** designing and building processes that better integrate participants and better facilitate iterative learning and improvement. The benefits of prefabrication and continual design and product improvement inherent in this type of systematic approach require the parallel systemization and continuity provided by some form of design-build or IPD method of project management. In a school-based project such as Refract House, it is most common to think of design-build as simply an organizational consequence of the school structure, in which the architecture and engineering students

also serve as the builders in order to get hands-on educational experience in the craft work. But this understanding is too narrow. Much more can be learned by the students, and offered to the industry as a whole, by recognizing that design-build cooperation and systemized fabrication and performance analysis are essential to understanding and designing the future of a creative architecture practice that would be fully engaged with the processes and opportunities of modern industrial production, and the increasingly complex and powerful digital tools of production and project management.

In the context of the Refract House project, prefabrication can be discussed on many levels, beginning with the obvious requirement for the home to be built in California, then trucked cross-country for a period of performance evaluation and exhibition in Washington DC, followed by a return to California and semi-permanent installation on the Santa Clara University campus. This is a fairly extreme example of off-site fabrication and modular relocateability, both because of the length of the 6,000-mile overland journey and because of the very short time allowance—just four days—from the moment of arrival in Washington DC to assembly and readiness for performance-monitored exhibition.

This engagement with prefabrication is straightforward to understand and explain (even while it is quite atypical of construction overall), as the three primary building-block components can be easily understood in diagrams and through seeing photos of the three largely complete modules traveling on three flatbed trucks. It also exemplifies a sequential design-build-install process of prefabrication that does not inherently involve the progressive learning resulting from a continuous engagement of the same design and production team throughout the project. While there were a good number of Refract House participants who stayed with the project from design through to the installation of the prototype in Washington DC, there was not an opportunity for utilizing the knowledge gained by the team in further iterations of the project overall.

To get beyond a conventional understanding of building prefabrication considered in terms of truck-size components, we should focus less on the last-stage joining of large-scale parts and more on the finer-grained process of modular design and construction that begins much earlier, in the conceptualization of the project, and continues as an organized process of development into serial learning applied to production of future component units.

For the students, instructors, and consulting professionals, one of the most exciting aspects of the Solar Decathlon is the chance to be engaged in truly cutting-edge design and process research in **BUILDING INFORMATION MODELING** a practically-applied project. Refract House and many other project entries over the history of the Solar Decathlon have actively embraced emerging solutions to energy and other building systems as well as the pragmatic need to integrate these technical advances with the needs of physical construction implementation, coupled with a balancing of demands related to budget, schedule, and performance evaluation context, and not least of all a comprehensive synthesis of architectural ambition. To best engage these issues and design opportunities, architecture will benefit from a broader concept of prefabrication and design-build team collaborations, and their relationship to iterative design and building information modeling (BIM).

In the design-build example of Refract House, the building was actually fabricated many times over the course of its creation, if one includes the numerous digital models of the design, all of the scale models that were built, the full-scale mockups of key elements and connections, and the sometimes ad-hoc, on-site revision and decision making that is seldom much acknowledged by architects but is always a major part of the process in any custom building project. Long before the Refract House team began building the final physical structure at the design-build site in Santa Clara, there had been an iterative process that allowed for a modeling of options and scenarios, often resulting in vigorous debate between the individual project participants, and the multiple subgroupings of the overall

ABOVE
View across ramp to the
Washington Monument

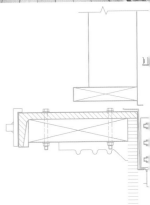

project team. The process wasn't always linear, and in some stretches it was downright messy, but in the end it not only led to a successful final product, but also provided some instructive insight into how we might better recognize and integrate this iterative component-based process of designing and making into our profession overall.

The two-year process of bringing Refract House from initial design studies to executed completion involved a very large number of individual contributors, each one of whom—as a student of architecture, engineering, or a related field—had the expected role and individual desire to shape the overall project in some identifiable way. By necessity of schedule, sequence, and practicality, these individual authors coalesced into working subgroups focused on different areas of the design, some studying in detail the gray-water recycling and planting systems, some the energy capture strategy, and some the interior finishes, lighting, and dinnerware. One of the most remarkable outcomes, and greatest collective achievements, was the degree to which these many subassemblies were successfully integrated into a relatively cohesive end product. In terms of visual design coherence, the interoperability of its technical systems, and the overall infusion of healthy, happy, lifestyle-focused ambiance that

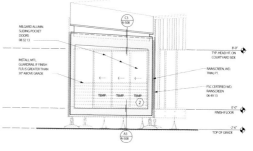

makes the house so attractive to occupy, Refract House is a triumph of ambitious design synthesis.

ABOVE
Glazed endcap of living room (module A)

While it wasn't explicitly structured as such, the Refract House project is an excellent example of the opportunities inherent in a design-build or Integrated Project Delivery (IPD) approach to INTEGRATED PROJECT DELIVERY architecture, in which a collaborative structure among all team members—architect, builder, owner—recognizes and facilitates the synergistic interdependence of contributions from all participants. This is quite distinct from the traditional design-bid-build construction sequence, which assumes a good deal of distance, and a linear relationship, between project participants. This traditional understanding of designer and builder relationships has long been the standard system of Western construction management, and too long and uncritically embedded as the most common premise in the structure of architectural education and professional practice.

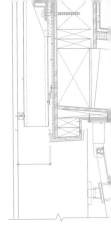

Refract House and the success of its multi-authored, component-based process can be used as an instructive model for future collaborative projects, particularly when viewed as the first stage in what would become a series of progressive and successive implementations. With an increasingly complex set of design problems to solve, and an increasingly rich and complex palette of materials and tools available to use in solving them, the role of collaborative, integrative, and iterative design processes should be more broadly considered as a fundamental basis for progress in architecture, and more explicitly embraced in architectural education and practice.

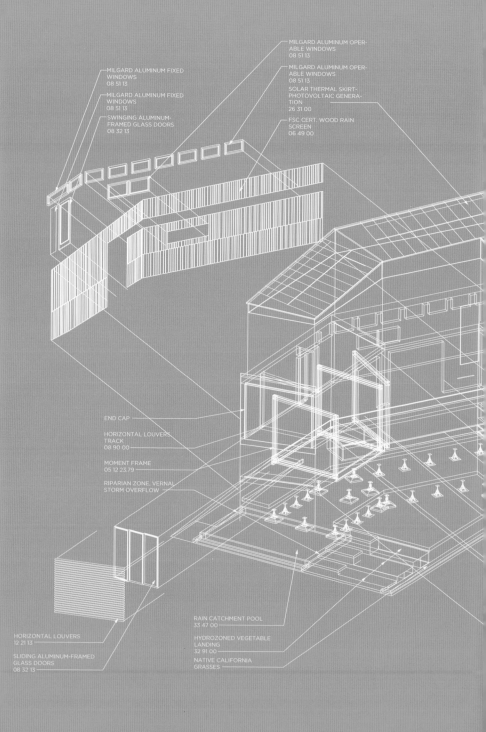

MILGARD ALUMINUM OPER-
ABLE WINDOWS
08 51 13

MILGARD ALUMINUM FIXED
WINDOWS
08 51 13

MILGARD ALUMINUM OPER-
ABLE WINDOWS
08 51 13

MILGARD ALUMINUM FIXED
WINDOWS
08 51 13

SOLAR THERMAL SKIRT-
PHOTOVOLTAIC GENERA-
TION
26 31 00

SWINGING ALUMINUM-
FRAMED GLASS DOORS
08 32 13

FSC CERT. WOOD RAIN
SCREEN
06 49 00

END CAP

HORIZONTAL LOUVERS
TRACK
08 90 00

MOMENT FRAME
05 12 23.79

RIPARIAN ZONE, VERNAL
STORM OVERFLOW

RAIN CATCHMENT POOL
33 47 00

HORIZONTAL LOUVERS
12 21 13

HYDROZONED VEGETABLE
LANDING
32 91 00

SLIDING ALUMINUM-FRAMED
GLASS DOORS
08 32 13

NATIVE CALIFORNIA
GRASSES

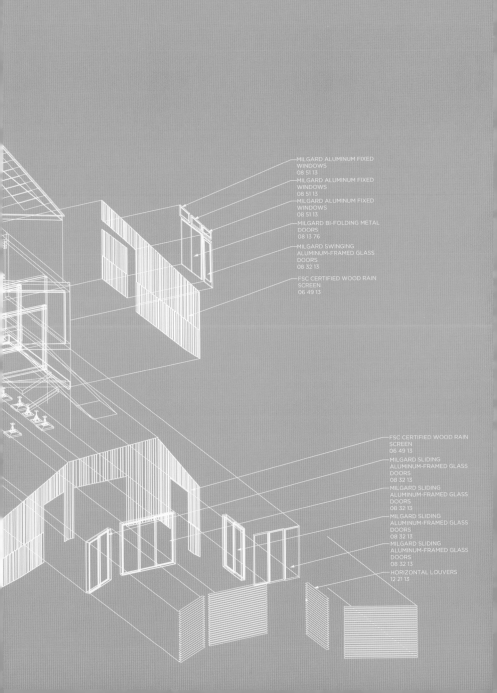

MILGARD ALUMINUM FIXED
WINDOWS
08 51 13

MILGARD ALUMINUM FIXED
WINDOWS
08 51 13

MILGARD ALUMINUM FIXED
WINDOWS
08 51 13

MILGARD BI-FOLDING METAL
DOORS
08 13 76

MILGARD SWINGING
ALUMINUM-FRAMED GLASS
DOORS
08 32 13

FSC CERTIFIED WOOD RAIN
SCREEN
06 49 13

FSC CERTIFIED WOOD RAIN
SCREEN
06 49 13

MILGARD SLIDING
ALUMINUM-FRAMED GLASS
DOORS
08 32 13

MILGARD SLIDING
ALUMINUM-FRAMED GLASS
DOORS
08 32 13

MILGARD SLIDING
ALUMINUM-FRAMED GLASS
DOORS
08 32 13

MILGARD SLIDING
ALUMINUM-FRAMED GLASS
DOORS
08 32 13

HORIZONTAL LOUVERS
12 21 13

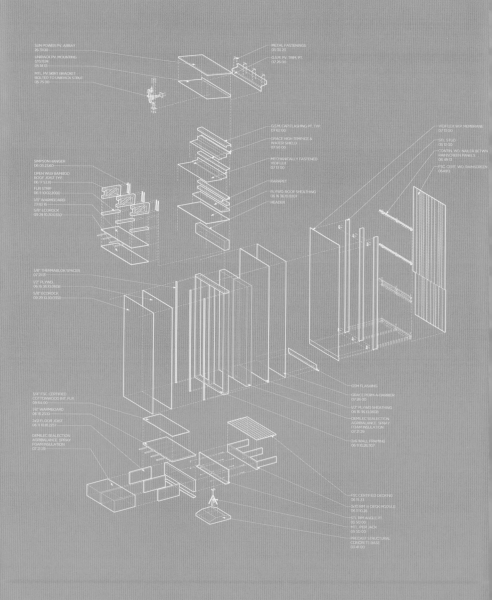

SUN POWER PV ARRAY
26 31 00

UNIRAC PV MOUNTING
SYSTEM
08 41 13

MTL PV SKIRT BRACKET
BOLTED TO UNIRAC STRUT
05 75 00

METAL FASTENINGS
05 05 23

G.S.M. PV TRIM PT.
07 26 00

G.S.M. CAP FLASHING PT. TYP.
07 62 00

GRACE HIGH TEMP ICE &
WATER SHIELD
07 90 00

MECHANICALLY FASTENED
VIOFLEX
07 13 00

PARAPET

PLYWD ROOF SHEATHING
06 16 36 10 0207

HEADER

VIOFLEX W.P. MEMBRANE
07 13 00

STL STUD
05 12 00

CONTINL WD. NAILER BETWN
RAINSCREEN PANELS
06 49 13

FSC CERT. WD. RAINSCREEN
06 49 13

SIMPSON HANGER
06 05 23 60

OPEN WEB BAMBOO
ROOF JOIST TYP.
06 17 53 10

FUR STRIP
06 11 10 02 2000

1/8" WARMBOARD
23 82 16

5/8" ECOROCK
09 29 10 30 0150

3/8" THERMABLOK SPACER
07 21 13

1/2" PLYWD.
06 16 36 11 0808

5/8" ECOROCK
09 29 10 30 0350

3/4" FSC CERTIFIED
COTTONWOOD INT. FLR.
09 64 00

1/8" WARMBOARD
06 16 23 10

2x12 FLOOR JOIST
06 11 10 06 2457

DEMILEC SEALECTION
AGRIBALANCE SPRAY
FOAM INSULATION
07 21 39

GSM FLASHING
07 26 00

GRACE PERM-A-BARRIER
07 26 00

1/2" PLYWD SHEATHING
06 16 36 11 0608

DEMILEC SEALECTION
AGRIBALANCE SPRAY
FOAM INSULATION
07 21 39

2x6 WALL FRAMING
06 11 10 26 307

FSC CERTIFIED DECKING
06 15 33

5x10 RIM @ DECK MODULE
06 11 10 26

STL RIM ANGLE PT.
05 50 00

MTL PIER JACK
05 50 05

PRECAST STRUCTURAL
CONCRETE BASE
03 41 00

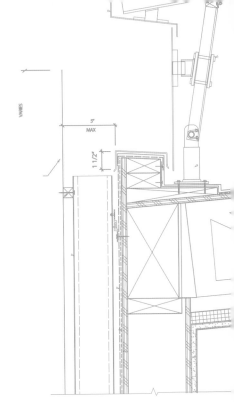

MATERIAL ASSEMBLIES
**MATT HUTCHINSON
& OBLIO JENKINS**

In an architectural project, the moment when drawing stops and building begins is never clear. The two are almost never mutually exclusive, and they continue simultaneously, either as generative or conceptual frameworks during early phases of design or as supplementary processes during fabrication and construction. But whatever the balance between drawing and making, there comes an inevitable point when it is necessary to begin to confront material reality.

For the students and faculty involved in Refract House, three semesters of planning and design work culminated in a moment when two critical shifts occurred. The first was a shift in modes of production, from a process primarily limited to drawing and modeling to one focused on making that involved physically testing previously developed ideas, with the end goal being the complete construction of the project. The second shift, necessitated by the first, was of a scalar nature, requiring not only different fabrication strategies for dealing with the impending realities of construction, but also a corresponding model

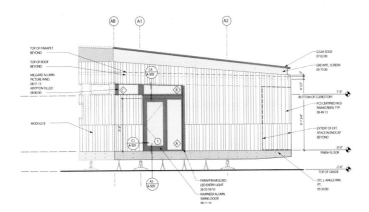

AB   A1   A2

TOP OF PARAPET
BEYOND
TOP OF ROOF
BEYOND
MILGARD ALUMIN.
PICTURE WND.
08 51 13
KRYPTON FILLED
08 80 00

MODULE B

G.S.M. EDGE
07 62 00
GKD MTL. SCREEN
05 75 00

7'-9"
BOTTOM OF CLERESTORY
FCS CERTIFIED W.D.
RAINSCREEN, TYP.
06 49 13
EXTENT OF EXT.
SPACE IN ENDCAP
BEYOND

0'-0"
FINISH FLOOR

-2'-6"
TOP OF GRADE

PARAFFIN MOLDED
LED ENTRY LIGHT
26 55 59.10
KAWNEER ALUMIN.
SWING DOOR
08 11 16

STL. L-ANGLE RIM,
PT.
05 50 00

of integrated thinking—an adaptable approach to dealing with materiality, ever-increasing detail, and multiple layers of assemblies.

With a fixed schedule and intensified pace of production during this transitional period, there was little time for critical evaluation or abstract debate over strategies and working methodologies. However, a retrospective investigation brings into focus several key issues that are worthy of discussion within a broader context. While these issues surfaced within an academic scenario, their relevance extends to anyone involved or interested in material culture and building production.

Looking back, three fundamental topics stand out. The first deals with materials and materiality itself. The second is concerned with the shaping, forming, and fabrication of component parts. The third builds on the first two and addresses communication conventions, issues of scale, and the logistics of system assemblies.

In his recent essay "Valuing Material Comprehension," James Carpenter makes a case for renewed exploration into materials knowledge, pointing out that "we cannot inhabit the world conceived in **MATERIAL STRATEGIES** a computer, however realistic it may appear."[1] There is no substitute for physical interaction with a concrete substance. This is especially poignant in the context of a design-build studio, where a certain level of material experimentation and research is an integral part of the design process, not just a supplement to it.

In the case of Refract House, however, and probably with many other types of building/making studios, a number of factors such as time constraints, access to appropriate facilities, and organizational structures contribute to the operation of "design" and "making" as two discrete phases. Unfortunately, the design phase usually takes precedence and the making is relegated to a supplementary role. This process is further complicated

ABOVE
North elevation of entry
module A

OPPOSITE
Salvaged redwood rain-
screen and clerestory

when the selection of materials, products, and systems must remain open-ended for longer than the normal duration because of the project's de-pendence on donated funds and materials, which may not be finalized until quite late in the project's development. How can architectural design, with the reality of construction at its core, operate effectively in these kinds of scenarios?

The answer may lie in examining different modes of material research: top-down formal strategies versus bottom-up material experimentation. Somewhat indicative of larger issues in the profession, where specialization has resulted in frag-

ABOVE
View of living room module from courtyard

OPPOSITE
Layered diagram of building cladding components and assembly

mented areas of knowledge, top-down strategies force architects to rely on technical experts and other outside consultants to imbue their "forms" with materiality. This mode of working can require compromising, even sacrificing, the initial design aspirations and material ambitions. In a best-case scenario it can lead to simplification and more efficient "refinement," but putting these questions in the hands of those with an agenda other than the architect's ultimately puts the overall design at risk.

Perhaps a more productive method is to integrate material research, testing, and experimentation from the beginning, developing material strategies that are integrated with the design itself, and intrinsically linking concept and intent with materiality and constructability. The architectural firm Barkow Leibinger, for instance, describes its own material research method as "a reversal of the normative design process: The starting point is a material, which leads to a detail, which leads to a prototype, which leads to program and siting." These architectural prototypes act as independent research, which can be folded into any number of design projects and "may or may not become a building."[2]

This model doesn't necessarily limit design flexibility; in fact it has the potential to allow more precise control and adaptability in the outcomes of various built designs. Synthesizing material strategies in parallel with design strategies means that knowledge of specific material production techniques (time, cost, limitations, et cetera) can be used to fine-tune or customize a solution without sacrificing intent. The more specific the designer's understanding of material attributes, the finer the control and mastery over fabrication variables, which allows a greater understanding of broader potential applications.

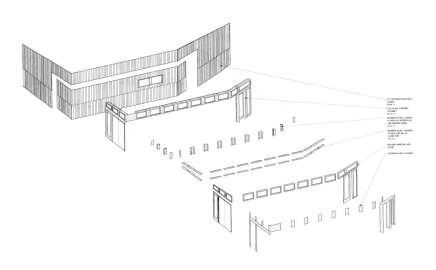

Working with even the most basic materials necessitates a keen understanding of the tools that shape them. In fact, material experimentation cannot be a fully successful endeavor without FABRICATION TECHNIQUES concurrently exploring the potentials of complementary fabrication processes. Just as learning the inherent qualities of materials results from experiencing them firsthand, an aptitude for making arises from trial-and-error exploration. Only so much fabrication intelligence (digital or analog—both are still physical acts) can be garnered from the computer's digital space. Simulation and virtual testing provide safety mechanisms to save time, material, and cost, but there comes the inevitable moment when the work must be outputted for physical scrutiny.

Ironically, the exactitude of computer modeling often encourages a false sense of completeness and accuracy, especially among students. While there may be a craft to digital modeling itself, it is not a replacement for true understanding of material and fabrication processes, which are dependent on direct experience. An example of this is building a digital model or assembly with zero tolerance built into or between components. While precision-machined parts might have a tolerance of a few hundredths of an inch or less, that variation is much larger for architectural systems. This variation must be built in, and it is extremely important in larger systems of assembly, but it ultimately begins with basic material units and knowledge

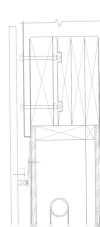

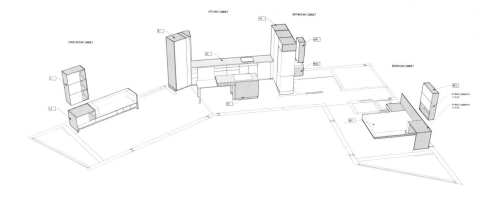

of fabrication techniques, for instance processes of subtraction (cutting, milling, punching), addition (casting, welding, stacking), forming (bending, pressing), and so on. Research into all kinds of processes will lead to a better understanding of machine (or labor) capacities, abilities, limitations, and tolerances. Those are closely and oftentimes directly related to material properties: graining, ductility, thermal expansion, et cetera.

The nuances of fabrication might not be readily apparent through computer modeling or even through singular prototyping; obtaining desired results or effects entails repeated empirical investigation. Expectations of exacting results or assumptions of successful prototyping without this procedure will only keep the quality of the work from progressing. The product developers of Panelite describe their process for working thus: "Multiple trials are necessary to determine whether a particular technique yields consistent results. . . . The iterative method allows for the occasional unexpected result, the 'error' in 'trial and error,' which may generate a separate productive line of research."[3] Within the controlled context of iterative experimentation, "errors" can even surface as productive diversions. Without serial testing, controlled variables are difficult to isolate and fruitful by-products are difficult to distinguish from pure accident.

This methodology does require time and foresight, luxuries not always possible in every project or situation. Students involved in the production of Refract House often had high ambitions for employing digital fabrication, only to find that without adequate time for testing, other fabrication strategies had to be explored. In the end, equivalent manual or analog "low-tech" techniques afforded greater built-in efficiencies (in other words, using stock solutions as opposed to custom solutions) that are often overlooked when pursuing a strictly digital agenda. The CCA Architecture students explored many solutions for the project's rainscreen enclosure,

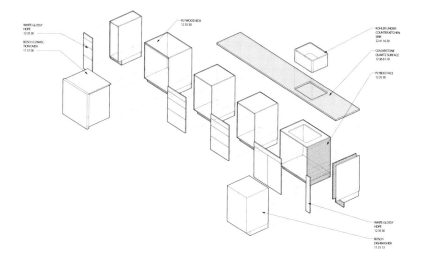

which would have used CNC-produced pieces to achieve random or gradient effects. In the end, simple salvaged redwood slats of various widths mounted on a Z-clip rail system achieved similar results without the need for additional fabrication.

An informed understanding of construction potential begins by working with base materials and honing fabrication techniques, and it is extended by the very nature of construction through incremental jumps of scale and complexity: from components to assemblies, systems of assemblies, and so on. The digital fabrication specialists designtoproduction describe their fundamental part-to-whole principles thus: "All architectural structures, unless dug into the earth, have this one thing in common: They are assemblies of numerous parts joined together. This statement is based on the simple fact that no single material, be it natural or manufactured, is as large as a building."[4]

From the smallest autonomous component to the largest prefabricated assembly, constraints on fabrication, transportation, and installation all limit constructability, which in turn affects the overall SCALES OF ASSEMBLY architectural intent. Of course this can vary greatly with building typology; whether it is prefabricated, site constructed, modular, or a prototype will impact decisions related to assembly logic. All of this suggests that the design process should encompass more than conceptual, formal, or programmatic development. It should also have embedded within it an organizational logic of assembly and construction. A top-down approach to making architecture without methods or layers of assembly built into the process proves difficult; it becomes a reverse-engineering exercise rather

ABOVE
Kitchen cabinet
component diagram

OPPOSITE
View of bathroom interior
with custom modular
components

than an inclusive and recursive process where all the constituent elements act as a comprehensive whole.

This is partly a matter of default practices and procedures, as standard architectural representations exist as abstractions of real material assemblies. Poché or abstractions of infill can serve as a stand-in for detail-to-come, although this leads to details being resolved ex post facto. Additionally, even the most descriptive wall section cannot convey all of the complexities inherent within a composite assembly. So, what might serve as the best way to conceptualize, develop, and communicate architectural assemblies?

The advantages of BIM (building information modeling) clearly provide at least a partial solution, serving as a collaborative database from which many parties can extract pertinent information. The concept of BIM challenges certain drawing conventions altogether, though its applicability for every type of scenario is debatable. In theory, this platform would be ideal in a design-build studio, allowing real-time design interaction between architecture and engineering students as well as fabricators and build-

ers. However, with the condensed timeframe for completing Refract House, the steep learning curve for proprietary software coupled with the constant turnover of students between semesters made it difficult to employ BIM as a design tool. While it was incorporated in aspects of Refract House, its role was reduced to compiling as-built documentation rather than enabling productive collaboration.

Another method for exploring and clearly communicating assembly logic and building system relationships is based on conventional construction documentation formats, but takes them further. Increasingly nonstandard approaches to design and fabrication require new hybrid forms of drawing sets that conflate design intent, detail and assembly logic, and explicit instructions. In 2000, SHoP Architects had the task of building their own design, *Dunescape*, the summer installation at P.S.1 in New York. They describe their workflow:

> "Rather than the traditional set of descriptive drawings, the construction documents were full-scale colour-coded templates for manufacture and assembly of the frames. The sim-

plicity of the system, comprising only two components (2x2 cedar sticks and 3-inch wood screws), fostered an accelerated learning curve, and construction was 'fast-tracked' with templates and materials for each day's work arriving on site as the installation progressed."[5]

Now even more than at that time, with the progression of technology and the increasing interoperability of software, individual drawings as well as entire document sets can be spliced together from any number of sources with the benefits of real-time updates between multiple parties and platforms. The contract document (CD) drawing set can include diagrams, plans, sections, details, axonometrics, perspectives, assembly instructions, cut lists, part indexes, and more. There are obviously certain standards that must be adhered to, but as each project is a unique assembly, there is no default method for describing and communicating every design.

In addition to drawing and modeling, and in order to facilitate a better understanding of materiality, scale, and the implications of design decisions, full-scale working mock-ups can prove invaluable for developing architectural systems. Students working on Refract House constructed a series of full-scale mock-ups of critical areas throughout the project, such as thresholds, connections between modules, and end conditions. When working at a 1:1 scale, unresolved details and discrepancies became immediately apparent. And these full-scale studies served as more than a simple means for investigating physical representations; they became platforms for debate and discussion.

ABOVE
View of kitchen with expandable dining room table

Producing architecture at any scale can be a complex endeavor, and it is tempting to simplify or isolate its processes into a step-by-step linear approach. Some processes are in fact inherently sequential NONLINEAR FEEDBACK and necessarily follow a specific order of operations. However, a simultaneous or synthetic approach that oscillates between design and making can provide a more extensive understanding of interrelated variables between part (material or component) and whole (architectural structure). A continuous, nonlinear feedback process that links thinking, drawing, and testing through making is the basis for holistically integrated solutions. No matter whether the context is an academic environment or professional architectural production, the outcome will exhibit a keener understanding of material potential and fabrication possibilities while also reinforcing the larger design intent.

NOTES   1. James Carpenter, "Valuing Material Comprehension" in *Building (in) the Future*, eds. Peggy Deamer and Phillip G. Bernstein (New York: Princeton Architectural Press, 2010): 64.

2. Frank Barkow and Regine Leibinger, *An Atlas of Fabrication* (London: AA Publications, 2009): 1.

3. Emmanuelle Bourlier, Andreas Froech, and Christian B. Mitman, "Material Effect" in *Versioning: Evolutionary Techniques in Architecture*, ed. Helen Castle (West Sussex, England: Wiley-Academy, 2002): 35.

4. Markus Braach, Fabian Sheurer, and Christoph Schindler, "The Whole and Its Parts" in *From Control to Design: Parametric/Algorithmic Architecture*, eds. Tomoku Sakamoto and Albert Ferré (New York: Actar-D, 2008): 161.

5. Chris William, Coren Sharples, Kim Holden, and Gregg Pasquarelli, "Eroding the Barriers" in *Versioning: Evolutionary Techniques in Architecture*, 91.

MATERIALS

BILLBOARDS: Salvaged billboards were used as exterior wall waterproof membranes. Normally a billboard is tossed after running its scheduled ad time. They are an excellent waterproofing material since they are U.V. resistant and able to shed water. Additionally, they accent the surface of the house underneath the rainscreen skin system.

THERMABLOK AEROGEL: To prevent energy loss due to thermal bridging, layers of ThermaBlok aerogel (which has a very low thermal conductivity) were placed between thermally active surfaces and steel moment frames. To prevent thermal bridging, a layer of ThermaBlok was added to all studs, essentially adding a layer of insulation to the house.

RECYCLED DENIM: Recycled denim is just as easy to use as conventional Batt insulation.

DERMILEC AGRIBALANCE INSULATION: Demilec Agribalance is a vegetable-oil-based sprayed foam insulation with excellent insulating properties.

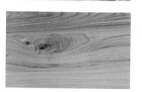

RECLAIMED ELM: The elm flooring used throughout the house is reclaimed from trees that died of Dutch Elm disease. Reclaimed elm also surfaces the central courtyard, reinforcing the continuity of the interior with the exterior of the house.

SALVAGED REDWOOD: The rainscreen is made of reclaimed California redwood acquired from local fire-damaged stock. A rainscreen is a simple siding system offset from the primary structure of the house that allows for ventilation, protects from driven drain, and minimizes thermal gain.

BAMBOO JOISTS: Innovative and sustainable open-web bamboo beams are the roof joists of the house. The beams provide structural support for the roof with minimal material and are open-web so that ducting, electrical wiring, and plumbing can be easily installed.

RECYCLED GLASS + SUSTAINABLE CERAMICS: The dinner set titled Green Ware was designed and crafted by Travis McFlynn. The material used includes a blend of local California clay mined near Sacramento called "Happy Clay." The glaze formulated for the ware consists of only three components: 70 percent recycled green tinted wine bottles ground in a ball mill to a fine powder called frit, 30 percent local clay, and boiled juice from the vegetable okra, added as a binder to make it more fluid during application. The clay and glaze were developed by John Toki, owner of Leslie Ceramic Supply Co.

LIGHTING & STRUCTURE

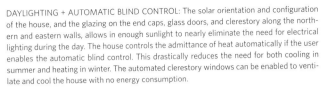

DAYLIGHTING + AUTOMATIC BLIND CONTROL: The solar orientation and configuration of the house, and the glazing on the end caps, glass doors, and clerestory along the northern and eastern walls, allows in enough sunlight to nearly eliminate the need for electrical lighting during the day. The house controls the admittance of heat automatically if the user enables the automatic blind control. This drastically reduces the need for both cooling in summer and heating in winter. The automated clerestory windows can be enabled to ventilate and cool the house with no energy consumption.

LED LIGHTING: All fixtures opt for LED lighting with low energy consumption, extremely long life, energy savings, and mercury-free construction. Outdoor lighting uses self-contained solar-powered lights by Meteor. These lights use the latest in solar cell LED lighting and ultracapacitor technology, characterized by lower energy consumption, safer walking spaces, and minimal maintenance for residents. Ultracapacitor units last as long as 10 years.

STRAW PENDANT: The Straw Pendant, made up of thousands of straws, was donated by Bay Area artist Dave Meeker.

LIGHTING CONTROLS: All wired lights are incorporated into the controls and monitoring system of the house. The system allows for both individual fixture adjustments as well as house-wide or area-specific lighting. Lights are controlled through LED panels and two-way switches located in each of the three modules. Residents have the option of remotely changing the lighting through an iPhone application specifically developed to control and monitor the systems of Refract House. This makes Refract House a "smart house," and the residents smart consumers.

STEEL ANGLE: The custom steel angle is the backbone of the house, transferring all gravity and lateral loads to the foundations. The angle provides a rigid support for the house and prevents it from buckling while allowing for the cantilevers of the endcaps. To form this angle, a large "C" channel shape (C15x50) was selected, and its top flange removed, leaving a tall, strong angle. The scrap material was reused in the base of the angle to provide a level support for the moment frames to sit on.

SEISMIC PIERS: Although the competition took place in Washington DC, where there is little to no seismic activity, the house was designed under the governing load case, which was at Santa Clara, California, where seismic activity is high. The project was designed using a seismically rated pier, giving the house a firm, safe, and modular foundation.

PREFABRICATED MODULES: The house is divided into three self-contained prefabricated modules for ease of transportation and assembly: entry/living room (module A), kitchen/bath (module B), and bedroom (module C).

MOMENT FRAME: To accomplish the feeling of openness throughout the building, moment frames were used to resist lateral loads in the transverse direction. The moment frames were designed to be as light as possible while still passing all governing seismic loading conditions. The walls had thin 2x6 framing so the columns of the moment frames would be as thin as possible, while deeper floor and roof joists allowed us to use deeper but lighter cross sections in the floor and ceiling. Furthermore, holes were strategically cut in the center of the webs of the moment frames to allow wires and pipes to easily pass through them later during construction.

THERMAL CONTROL & MONITORING

HYDRONIC SYSTEM: The energy for Refract House's conditioning was transferred by water through a hydronic system piping network. All equipment, pumps, and controls were engineered to use as little energy as possible, while delivering exactly the prescribed water temperature to ensure optimum system performance.

AIR-TO-WATER HEAT PUMP: The heating and cooling of Refract House is accomplished with a super-high-efficiency (18 SEER) air-to-water heat pump chiller that uses electricity to move heat from the outside air to water, or vice versa. Water is then pumped to the radiant system and fan coil unit to condition the house. RECIRCULATION PUMP: A recirculation pump is used to drain lukewarm water in the hot water line and replace it with hot water. To reduce the energy consumption, a motion sensor is coupled with the pump to start circulating water when someone enters the bathroom.

RADIANT COOLING + HEATING: Radiant heating is a comfortable, efficient, and healthy technology that saves energy and keeps residents more comfortable because it radiates directly to the occupants. The lack of a large blown-air system also reduces dust and contaminants and keeps the house quiet. Refract House employs this same technology for both heating and cooling. The radiant heating and cooling system operates through hot or chilled fluid that moves through the ceiling and floor of the house. These pipes are routed in Warmboard, a subfloor that is designed for homes using radiant conditioning.

SEASONAL BUFFER TANK: The thermal system employs a seasonal buffer tank that is kept cool during the summer months and warm during the winter months, allowing instant delivery of heating and cooling. The buffer allows the system to run the heat pump when it is most efficient during the day, or when electricity rates are low, to save money and promote grid health.

OUTDOOR VENTILATION + ERV: Refract House uses a small blown-air system to complement the radiant system with dehumidification, fresh air, and additional heating and cooling. This system features smart controls that enable optional energy recovery (pre-heating/cooling and humidifying/dehumidifying of incoming air with exhaust air) and mechanical ventilation (where cool air is brought in without conditioning to cool the house) when conditions make it favorable.

CONTROL SYSTEMS: The heating, cooling, ventilation, hot water, and fenestration systems are controlled by an Uponor Network Control system. This system is engineered to allow the user complete control of his or her environment, including temperature, humidity, and CO_2/VOC levels, all remotely via a web interface. System information is displayed via the house energy monitoring system. The home's temperature can be programmed from a student-designed iPhone app, the home's touchscreen, or a website.

ENERGY-SAVING WEATHER MONITORING: The monitoring system provides details on energy saved by the house's thermal systems compared to a conventional system, and detailed data on the heat supplied to the home. It includes a home weather system providing information on temperature, humidity, wind speed and direction, and rainfall. The system determines the efficiency of the solar panels and informs the control system if it starts raining. The weather station can measure rainfall intensity (rainfall per square foot), generating an approximate amount of the total rainwater catchment harvested in the reflecting pool.

HOMEOWNER INTERFACE: Building Dashboard® provides a system to easily view monitoring data by combining different engineering systems into one usable platform. The data posted on a website allows homeowners to select units of water and energy consumption by providing current home conditions, historical data, helping identify lifestyle trends and improvements. Monitoring data can be accessed through the Refract House iPhone application. With help from members of the University of Santa Clara's 2007 Solar Decathlon team each system was networked through the Cisco® Network Building Mediator.

PHOTOVOLTAIC SYSTEM: The Sunpower 225 solar panels were selected because of their high efficiency of 18.1 percent and peak output of 225 watts. The black finish and unique racking system integrated the solar panels into the roof system.

SOLAR RAKING SYSTEM: Using SolarMount rails and Unirac standoffs, the array spans all three modules of the house with one continuous plane. The panels are matched up to the edges of the building and the array angle is only raised to 10.5 degrees. The sides of the array are covered by a mostly opaque screen in order to hide all of the supports for the elevated array and provide the visual impression of a single roof.

POWER INVERTER: The SMA Sunnyboy Inverter was deployed in the house because of its high-efficiency inversion process. The inverters convert the harvested direct current solar energy to alternating current consumed by appliances. The SMA Sunnyboy is one of the highest-rated inverters on the market today.

MAIN CIRCUIT BREAKER: The Powerlink G3 3000 Lighting Control System is the main circuit breaker implemented in the house. The Powerlink controls all circuits through the internet. Residents can easily access the lighting control system and initiate overrides, turn off unnecessary lights, and cease vampire loads.

RAINWATER HARVESTING + GPLANT: Refract House harvests its rainwater runoff. The reflecting pool is the collection area for the rainwater, making it both an aesthetic and sustainable feature. The gray water is filtered by a passive plant system called the GPlant. The system is composed of five layers: loam, sand, gravel, biomatrix, geotextile. Each layer filters specific components out of the gray water. The processed gray water, termed recycled water, is used for irrigation.

PLANT SCHEDULE: The plant schedule includes an edible vegetable garden and natives such as the Showy Fridge Pod, Soaproot, Turkey Mullien, Nodding Beggartick, Willow Dock, Checkerbloom, Clover, Spikerush, Folded Calico-Flower, Narrow-Leaved Cattail, Slender Hairgrass, Water Plantain, White Navarretia, Dwarf Sack Clover, Vernal Pool Buttercup, Vernal Pool Goldfield, Field Owl's Clover, Woolly Marbles, Ropevine, Field Sedge, and Brown Dogwood.

SMART IRRIGATION MANAGEMENT: Refract house uses the WeatherTRAK Smart Controller. WeatherTRAK adjusts watering according to local weather, using weather satellites to determine current and forecasted conditions.

WATER MONITORING: Metrics about the Refract House's water use are featured on the building dashboard, built by Lucid Design. The dashboard depicts information gained via flowmeters about potable water consumption, wastewater generation, gray water generation, shower hot water use, shower cold water use, and irrigation usage.

This publication was sponsored by a grant from the Pacific Gas and Electric Corporation Foundation, whose funding is dedicated to education and environmental stewardship. Many thanks to Stephen Beal, president of California College of the Arts, and F. Noel Perry, chair of the CCA Board of Trustees, for their enthusiastic support of Refract House and the Solar Decathlon competition. This project was made possible by Ila Berman, director of Architecture and editor of the CCA Architecture Studio Series at California College of the Arts.

PROJECT CREDITS

ARCHITECTURE

CALIFORNIA COLLEGE OF THE ARTS ARCHITECTURE FACULTY AND STUDENTS:
Director of Architecture: Dr. Ila Berman
Faculty:
Architectural design: Andrew Kudless
Design development / project management: Kate Simonen, Peter Anderson, Oblio Jenkins, Matt Hutchinson
Interior Design: Bruce Levin
Architecture student team: Blake Altshuler, Ronald Arana, Frank Baumgartner, Kyle Belcher, Allison Buggs, Yoon Choi, Chris Chalmers, Woojin Chung, Cristian Cortes, John Hobart-Culleton, Diana De la Torre, Laurice der Bedrossian, Loi Dinh, Chris Gardini, Charles Goodnight, Noah Greer, Jenny Guan, Patrick Herald, Mariah Hodges, Madeline Honig, Brandon Jenkins, Alvin Kong, Darlene Kong, Olga Kozachek, Gabrielle Kupfer, Anna Leach, Wayne Lin, Ryan Linkey, Mason Liskamm, Sandra Lopez, Mariko Low, Jonathan Manzo, Justin Mason, Annessa Mattson, Tan Nguyen, Michael Perkins, Andrew Peters, Annabel Peterson, Doug Ponciano, Aaron Poritz, Walter Ramos, David Rodriguez, Ocean Rogoff, Ricardo Ruiz, Michelle Santos, Raphael Stargrove, Andrew Stolz, Devi Sundararaman, Paul Taylor, Angela Todorova, Bret Walters, Felix Wang, Amy Wazni, Olesya Yefimov, Min Chin Yi, Maryam Zahedi
Interior Design: Jackie Morck, Larry Peifer

GRAPHIC DESIGN

CALIFORNIA COLLEGE OF THE ARTS GRAPHIC DESIGN FACULTY AND STUDENTS:
Faculty: Cinthia Wen, Steve Lyons
Graphic Design student team: Tim Gruneisen, Leah Hickey, Mike Hu, Heidi Reifenstein, Lucinda Waysack, Brad Wharton, Siming Wong
CCA student contributions: Furniture: Jeremy Kaplan; Industrial Design: Ryan Francis, Lily Kolle Kahle-Riggs; Ceramics: Travis McFlynn; Glass / lighting fixtures: Matty Harvey, Paul Taylor; Textiles: Alexandra Milukhin; Fine Arts: Alicia Escott, Julia Goodman, Grady Gordon, Sarah Hobstetter; Fashion Design: Lauren Devenney, Victoria Anne Dickson, Sam Forno, Mai Nguyen, Crystal Titus, Zahra Tyebjee; Film/videography: Alex Winter

ENGINEERING

SANTA CLARA UNIVERSITY ENGINEERING FACULTY AND STUDENTS:
Faculty: Dr. Tim Hight, Dr. Mark Aschheim, Father Jim Reites, Dr. Tim Healy
Student team:
Structural engineering /construction: Jeff Abercrombie, Spencer Ambauen, Ashley Cigiar, Erica Fieger, Steven Hight, Sean Irwin, Brian Reeves, Dan Ruffoni, Mike Sizemore, Andrew Smith, Stoney Strickland, Mikell Warms, Felipe Yerkes Medina

Electrical/mechanical engineers: Hazella Bowmani, Matt Brubaker, Collin Lee, Richard
Navarro, Ross Ruecker, Jeff Seago, Tim Sennott, Mike Vlahos
Other: Caitlyn Alexander, Preet Anand, Ryan Diemer, Allison Kopf, Kadee Mardula, Tori
Watson
Contractor/manufacturer: construction by SCU students
Subcontractors: Summer & Sons Electric, Milgard Windows, Vertex Electric,
Cupertino Electric
Additional consultants: Ryan & Associates, Stan Wu, Steve Brody, Steve Ashford,
Hallmark Construction, Pasha

COMMUNICATIONS AND PUBLIC RELATIONS
Brenda Tucker (CCA) and Connie Coutain (SCU)

AWARDS
AIASF Special Achievement Award
NCARB Prize
National Building Museum Honor Award

SUPPORT
Major project funding: U.S. Department of Energy, Applied Materials, Bank of America,
searchcafe, Pacific Gas and Electric Company, Michael Lee Environmental Foundation,
Hallmark Construction, Pasha, Webb Family Charitable Foundation, Teragren, Valence
Energy, Santa Clara University, Lucid Design Group, National Semiconductor, Regrid
Power, Demilic, Next 10, Summers & Sons Electric Inc., Uponor, Ideate, Warmboard,
Meteor, Ryan & Associates, Silicon Valley Power, Pine Cone Lumber, Bendheim, Juno
Lighting Group, Milgard

PUBLICATION CREDITS
Editors: Ila Berman and Nataly Gattegno
Faculty contributors: Ila Berman, Nataly Gattegno, Andrew Kudless, Tim Hight, Kate
Simonen, Peter Anderson, Matt Hutchinson, Oblio Jenkins
Design: CCA Sputnik / Suzanne Baxter and Jason Kerr
Faculty advisor: Bob Aufuldish
Design manager: Steven Spingola
Managing editor: Lindsey Westbrook
Photographer: Cesar Rubbio
Printer: Regal Printing Ltd., Hong Kong
Print advisor: Celeste McMullin

This book is part of the CCA Architecture Studio Series of publications. It documents student and faculty
work from the advanced architecture studios supporting the development of Refract House, a two-year
collaborative project between the Division of Architecture at California College of the Arts and the School of
Engineering at Santa Clara University.

ISBN 978-0-9825033-2-4